Search For Light

Claus Hackenberger

Book Publishers Network

Book Publishers Network
P.O. Box 2256
Bothell • WA • 98041
P<small>H</small> • 425-483-3040
www.bookpublishersnetwork.com

Some events in this book did not pass the way the author reports them. But some of his stories describe real happenings life presents. Any reference to businesses, organizations, and locales are intended only to give the fiction a sense of authenticity. Any resemblance to actual persons, living or dead, remains entirely coincidental.

Copyright 2009 by Claus Hackenberger
Author of A LONG WALK and *the river*
P.O. Box 2254, Renton, WA 98056
www.claushackenberger.com

All rights reserved. No part of this publication, drafts and/or excerpts, may be reproduced or transmitted in any form or by any means, electronic or mechanical, including photocopying, recording, or any information storage retrieval system, without permission in writing from the author.

Library of Congress Number: 2008906444
ISBN10: 1-887542-87-6
ISBN13: 978-1-887542-87-6
Manufactured in the United States
10 9 8 7 6 5 4 3 2 1

Editor: Vicki McCown
Cover Artwork: Claus Hackenberger
Cover Design: Laura Zugsda
Book Design: Stephanie Martindale
Artwork by the Author
Graphic clipart © 2009 Jupiterimages Corporation

Also by

Claus Hackenberger

A LONG WALK

and

the river

*to all of my friends, to my family, to the past,
to tomorrow
in peace and in love*

*stashed with these pages you find
thoughts you might like to explore*

Now
Tomorrow
Hard times
Beautiful moments
Sunrise
Love
Forgiving
Peace
God
Tears
Laughter
Happiness
Longing
Life

Index on page 149

Acknowledgments

Without the help and encouragements of my friends I could not have undertaken to write this third book of mine.

Gail Beck, Sheila Curwen, Denny Sather, Candy Cullen, and Roxann Genzale, you readers lent your critique and offered your suggestions. Please, accept my heartiest thanks.

Yet even the best content may not ray from shelves unless a book's packaging and design attracts people's curiosity. Laura Zugsda, with your cover, and Stephanie Martindale, with your arrangement of this book you did outstandingly well. I do thank you!

Though, to make syntax jive, to make my writing readable, to make the lines flow, to convey meaning and mood, my editor, Vicki McCown, touched every letter, every dot with her wand. Without her work, her input, my stories would be nothing but pebbles somewhere in the sand. Vicki, thank you.

And you, Sheryn Hara, my publisher, you brought my work to the market place, thank you, thank you all.

Prologue
Changing Tides

A weary day dims its light. Soon dusk will call the dark to settle over pastures, between the trees of the nearby forest, and around our homes. A soft blanket, thin fog sways with the curling waters, the river pushes toward the lake. The wind, its bluster spent, hides somewhere to rustle up strength for tomorrow's challenge.

Ebb tide, down along the shore, the receding ocean leaves a wide beach, empty of people, naked, saddening. Small crabs scurry sideways over the dark sand; further out, kelp tails slither back and forth as if they were snakes. A few unseen clams shoot water straight up into the tangy air, short-lived candles sculpted of liquid glass. Barnacles, gray-white, cluster over rocks strewn about.

Rain, a while back, had soaked the driftwood to its core. The log I usually rest on shows standing water in the dents the sea has carved during its long journey, maybe from the Far East, maybe from farther away yet.

Here I render my world. I feel God near. I find it easy to pray, to ask, to listen, to think.

Back, long ago in the past, drowned in aloneness, hurting, I often fled to this place. And sometimes I did ask the tide to take me to sea. I argued with the Lord, dared Him in shameful arrogance.

I wanted someone to love me. I wanted to be where rainbows are born, to go to where no weekdays live between Sundays. I wanted to stop drinking, stop to cry. I wanted my friends back. I wanted so much, yet I had nothing to give.

I now can touch my past. I do not hurt anymore.

Claus Hackenberger

Search for Light

I DO NOT BELIEVE IN ACCIDENTS; RATHER DO I THINK ALL MOMENTS, BUILDING OUR TIME, ARE ESSENTIAL, MEANINGFUL MESSAGES FROM WHICH LIFE LETS US CHOOSE. AND EVERY SO OFTEN ONE OF THOSE MOMENTS COMES ABOUT ALL COVERED WITH GLITTER FROM STARS YONDER OUR REACH, WAKING OUR SOUL, HAVING US DARE TO BE.

From a letter to someone I care about

Littleman

The year is two thousand and eight. The past already has gobbled up over half of it. Summer flowers bloom all over, wake dawns lusting for life.

Yes, the tides still come and go, play at the shore. I never tire of wandering along that narrow strip where land and ocean meet. I walk, I dream, I pray. Early this morning, I took my little dog to the beach at Seahurst Park, a short half hour from where we live. Both of us like this beach. I let him run without his leash. He is eager to find his special spots amidst twisted drifted wood.

I watch him go and remember.

My son and his family had invited me to visit their Denver home between Christmas Day and New Year, 2005. Misha picked me up at the airport. Bright sun, blue sky, the snow-capped Rocky Mountains along the western horizon, the vast desert to the east—these conspired to zoom my little Renton-Town way out of reach.

Barely did we get home, when Micki, Misha's wife, urged me into their spacious living room.

"Wait a minute. My shoes are wet with snow," I protested.

"Quick, take 'em off and sit down on that couch over there."

Heavy expectations bounced off the walls. Funny grins masked the faces hanging out in that living room.

Carrie, my granddaughter, her lovely face beaming, said her greetings, but skipped the hug as she placed a fairly large Christmas-dressed box on the coffee table in front of me. It glittered with colorful wrapping paper held together by ribbons and bows.

"Wow, what is it?"

Stupid question, I know.

"You must open it to find out. But please be careful, Opa. It's very fragile."

I stood up and with extreme caution started to undo the beautiful dressings. Then the lid came off. The box, for all I could see, looked to be empty. Then in one corner I spied a small black and fuzzy ball.

Afraid to touch it, I looked at my granddaughter, silently asking for some guidance.

Suddenly, the black piece of fur moved.

"Take it out," Carrie commanded.

I did. The "ball" was alive. I saw it had a tiny head between two large flopping ears. White mini-teeth showed as it opened its tiny mouth and began to lick my hand. Black eyes, black pearls, shiny little black stars looked at me,

My eyes went wet.

A dog! I h a v e a d o g !

I remember holding my dog, my fuzzy thing, like I would have held a raw egg outside its shell.

Warm. He felt so warm.

"He's a toy poodle," said Carrie. "The breeder named him 'Littleman,' but you can change it if you want."

"Littleman," I said, falling into those dark pools with which he looked at me.

The name fit into my mouth perfectly.

*T*he security checks at the airport posed no problem. "Sir, what's in the—Oh, my God! George, Pat, come look at what we have here."

They asked me to take him out of the carrying case and walk through the magnetic frame with him.

"Is that thing real?"

"It's so sweet, can I hold it too?"

"Oh my Lord, I never saw anything so cute."

By that time the whole line of passengers, smiling, waiting, waved at us.

Boarding the plane, I walked right by the greeting flight attendants and found my seat, 18 C. No alarms went off, no buzzers rang. Carefully, I pushed the case under the seat in front and pretended I was traveling alone.

You see, I had not paid for him. A woman in the waiting area had put fear into my head. She warned I would be charged double for my deception.

A frightened yelp escaped from under the seat in front of me exactly as a stewardess passed by.

"Did you hear that?"

I tried to make my face say, "Who, me?" But my heart interrupted.

"It's my Christmas present from my granddaughter," I volunteered.

She wore a smile on her lips as she moved on down the aisle, closing overhead bins.

Once airborne, I took Littleman from his prison and let him settle on my lap. He licked my hand.

"I love you too," I whispered.

Within a couple of months, Littleman and I settled into our life together, comfortable, happy, well-matched.

And yet…I still marvel at how he had walked into my space through an opening I did not know was available to him. In such a short time, he had become a most important thread in my life's tapestry. So much more than a cute ball of fur to be patted, hugged, indulged at my whim, Littleman lets me see in him a unique and precious life that reaches out to touch my reality. It is not I who owns him only; he wants and needs to own a part of me too. He allows me to feel the beauty he holds inside, the essence of Littleman that he shields with his pearl-black eyes.

Perhaps this is why I see less of an animal in him, and more of a sentient being, one to whom I can respond on a higher level.

I wonder how a girl who lives over a thousand miles away found a tiny creature who fit so perfectly with this old man.

Thank you always for that small miracle, Carrie Anne.

If I Could Write

Renée—

Thinking of you, dreaming, in silence speaking your name, listening to your voice, kissing your eyes, embracing you, feeling warmth…

Let me tell of some sweet poetry I once heard many years ago.

Just for a moment, imagine I could reach beyond the clouds and borrow a little blue from the sky to use for ink in my pen.

I'd write, my words carefully built, would address you humbly. Angels, violins, and cellos I'd ask to serenade. Earth would stop to turn while you listened.

But I know, all the blue I could have fetched would hardly be enough to write "I love you." Because I'd paint these letters so tall they would pierce the sky.

Please, accept these smaller fonts. I will make sure they do touch heaven.

Search for Light

SMALL STEPS CAN COVER LONG DISTANCES.

Talking to myself

A Few Days Before Christmas

Often book stores will invite me to bring my books and set up shop for a day. These "book signings," as they are called, have always brought such wonderful opportunities to connect with others. A few words, a handshake or a hug, and an instant bond is forged, a melding of mind, soul, and heart.

Two such occasions have touched me deeply.

The first occurred some years back, a few days before Christmas, at The Book Store in Tukwila. Judd, the store manager, had arranged for my display table to sit right at the entrance to this large store. Busy, very busy, and yet he helped me with the setup of my books. Martha, a bookseller, brought a bouquet of Christmas flowers.

Standing there for eight hours being a salesman took all the steam I could simmer. But I liked promoting my work this way. Talking to so many people, offering compassion, speaking of peace, of freedom, of love and forgiveness, listening to young and old, their astonishment or disappointment—never in my life have I found such great reward for whatever I had to share.

*A*h, the Christmas season. The store bristled with holiday shoppers, gleamed with colorful, glittering decorations. The ceiling came alive with ribbons, garlands, bows, streamers. Festive music softly mingled with the rumble of the roaming people.

Outside, snow drifted silently, white-washed streets, trees, and the many parked cars. Everybody shook their coats and stomped their feet on the carpet as they entered the store.

The staff wore Sunday clothes, throwing out answers to questions that flew from every direction. The traffic at the cashier registers was heavy, rush hour all over.

The long bookracks strained under the load of paper weight and the enormous wisdom dripping from the pages.

In this friendly chaos I kept signing books while never quite able to finish my presentational for the bystanders.

Every once in a while, Judd came and pointed his two thumbs straight up in the laden air. A kind man, he also brought ice cold water to keep my voice from fading away.

My cheeks began to hurt, not used to holding my smile all day long. Saying this I don't mean to be funny. I know of no other way to convince people I am thankful for their interest in my writing. They do deserve a kind smile, my thanks and assurance of their decision to accept what I am offering.

*B*ethlehem came up in my thoughts. I began to feel a little festive myself. It did not last.

The boy was about twelve. The mother walking aside him could have been in the midst of her fourth decade. Both had their hands on the crossbar of the wheelchair they were pushing. The man in that wheelchair wore a blanket over his lap. I did not see his legs. They were not there.

The three hesitated. I greeted them and handed over a copy of A LONG WALK.

"You are Claus? You wrote this the book? WW II, Hitler, and so on?"

"Yes, sir, I am talking of my life during those infamous years."

"I'm Mark, my wife, Lynn, and my boy, Man."

"Good to meet you all…"

They listened to my presentation. He looked at me, and I felt his pain racing through my heart.

"I would like to buy your books. Could you sign them, please, and dedicate both to my wife and my son? They are my heroes."

Like he needed to explain, to apologize, he said,

"Soon I will get new legs. I will work them hard to get me to walk away from Iraq."

God, why do you let this happen?

I signed and wrote,

Mark and Lynn and Man,

Thank you for sharing with me your love for each other
I pray for you to keep Peace living in your hearts.

The day moved on. Judd bustled about, refurbishing my table with books to replace those that had gone out the door. A middle-aged man entered the store. He came straight to me, grabbed a copy from the stack of A LONG WALK, ripped the book open, and after having read the jacket he asked,

"Did you write this stuff?"

Strange, after over several years, four thousand copies, and talking to hundreds and hundreds of people—for the first time, a customer, this man, made me feel uncomfortable.

"Yes, sir, it is my autobiography, during World War II."

"I assume you wrote for Hitler, you supported him…"

"No. Sir, do you know what it means to have grown up during that horrific time?"

"Hah, you were a lucky boy."

"How so?"

"Hitler was a good man, yes! He did a lot of good things. Despite that there are so many fucking liars around telling that shit about the ovens and all that other crap."

What am I going to do? The soldier from Iraq had left. Thank the Lord, no chance for his family to hear this. I hid my hands deep in the pockets of my trousers, not for this jerk to see them shake. Don't blow it, Claus, don't.

"Sir, if that's what you think, it is you who is lying. I lived there, trust me, I know."

"Hey, author, **you** are not telling the truth, shithead."

Passersby hesitated, not certain what to think. But I somehow succeeded to disarm their worry.

"Please, man, put this book back. I did not write it for you."

I made sure my hands, probably white-knuckled fists by then, stayed in my pockets. He kept on, shouting now.

"The whole story about burning the Jews…that Auschwitz crap is all a big lie."

Seldom has other people's hate affected me so deeply. He threw the book back onto the table. It bounced off and landed on the floor behind me. A young boy picked it up and brought it back.

I worked on letting my fists go open. God, how could we work on this man's face to do away with that hate in his restless eyes? I ended up, though, praying for him. And once in a while I still do.

Judd came and looked at me with concern.

"You okay?"

I remember the slow nod of mine.

An elderly lady approached from the magazine racks, halted at my table, hung her cane over the edge and let her purse rest on top of *the river*.

Now what?

"Hi, Claus, I read your books. I came by to thank you in person for you having the courage to tell about your life, your joy, and your pain. Thank you."

Now, this was different. My *Angelus Domini* must have sent her. I motioned to say something, but she raised her hand ever so slightly and kept on.

"Claus, I heard this man talking to you. What he said did hurt, hurt me."

She came around and stopped right in front of me.

"You know, Auschwitz, the ovens did burn, still do. All still is as it has been ever since. They will be burning as long as we live."

My God!

With her right hand she opened the button on the sleeve of her left arm and rolled it up some. She then turned her lower arm a little outward and held it up. I saw the blue tattooed number German SS-men had burned into her flesh. I could not keep in my tears.

"Claus, I am a proud Jewish woman, you must be a proud Christian. You need to know, you must know, I have forgiven all of it. And today on your Christmas, I want to renew this commitment. I am praying that we forgive ourselves and others."

"Thank you! I know, without forgiving no love can be born and grow. No new day will happen. I will guard this moment never to be lost. Thank you."

She asked could she give me a hug. I wanted to grab her. I needed her touch, her warmth, her past. I wanted to feel her pain, her despair, her courage. I wanted to kiss those who set her free.

We hugged, did not let go for a while.

I never expected any such a deep-soul moment would come to life by the words and thoughts I share.

Throughout the years as I kept promoting my books, other great moments came to life, begging to stay with me for time to come.

These moments confirmed my belief in people. Again and again, old and young allowed me to touch their inner softness, their soul. Humble and sincere, they offered their skills, wanting to be involved with making a difference. I found them craving for peace and goodness. Book signings were and still are a blessing to me.

I did not know this when I filled the first pages of my work. Writing to me became sharing a passing on of hope, yes, and feelings of pain and laughter.

*I*n Silverdale, Washington, I was allowed to be a witness to life bursting with love.

I must tell.

Halfway through my shift, a middle-aged couple came and listened to my short speech. I could see the husband wanted a copy of A LONG WALK. His woman caressed the cover of *the river*. They talked. The woman smiled, nodding. I signed A LONG WALK for him. He gave her a kiss and both headed for Starbucks at the other end of the store.

A little later, while I was busy with other prospective buyers, that man came back and waited for me.

"Yeah, Mister Claus, *the river*, please. I want to surprise her. Would you sign it too and add something like 'good luck' or so? You know, she is so very ill…"

His eyes went wet. I signed and did what he had asked me for. He returned to the latte shop. Soon thereafter I saw them leaving. The man, with his arm around her waist, waved.

I said a Hail Mary for them.

On a mental break, drinking ice water, I saw that same woman rushing back into the store.

"Claus, sitting in the car, I read your bio. I also have cancer. It is not sleeping like yours. My God, I want you to hug me."

We embraced. And then she removed from her sweater what I saw was some trinket.

"Here, Claus, please, I want you to have this. A friend gave it to me wishing it would help me fight. God bless you. See you in heaven?"

She put her hand to her face, turned, and left me standing in awe, not knowing what to do.

The "trinket" turned out to be an angel, an inch-tall, well-worn, here and there still showing its gold in the folds of his porcelain gown. His wings were spread. He had only one foot left, the other one lost along his journey. But I checked—all the other things angels have and usually do, most likely still were working.

Making my way home, I went to see a friend who only had a short time left before her cancer would still her heart. I gave her the angel.

"Sandy, he just might have a message for you. He had one for me."

She looked at the angel with eyes that were preparing to see God.

I asked all angels to help her on the way to heaven.

Christmas

Colored lights everywhere—dressing windows, strung on trees, draped along eaves, dangling from gables of homes on either side of the street I live on—lure me into a festive mood.

Even fences are decorated with tiny twinkling stars. The fir branch I broke from a tree in my yard spreads its needle-green fragrance from my kitchen into the living room, all through the house. The smell of steaming coffee sneaks by. Two candles flicker where I sit and write. My place is warm, cozy, still. So am I.

Two thousand years have gone by since that night in Bethlehem. As long as I can remember I have tried to understand the message those shepherds heard. Judea now drenched in blood suffers with unrest, violence, and death. Killings have become common events.

The older I get, the more hollow this "Merry Christmas" sounds. More, though, does Christmas ask than just to be merry, to have peace. We must believe in peace and love, constantly renew our commitment to these ideals, take those actions throughout the year that make peace the way in which we live each and every day.

The burned houses in Kosovo are cold and stand black against the western sky. Snow covers blood and graves. Weeping children twist branches into wreaths and hang them over makeshift crosses. Those children, their bleeding souls miss their mothers. Whole villages have been erased from the land. I know just "Merry Christmas" will not do.

I pray for them.

And I wish that, beyond the Hallelujahs of this Holy Night, they and you and I may find—no, that *we* bring about—the peace we are longing for.

Peace

Bethlehem

I remember, celebrate the supreme
event when man received grace
to weave a new fabric into life

whoever let us find love and
forgiveness also brought heaven
closer to earth

we believe or we might not ... still
Stable and Star and Shepherds
will stay with us

At Safeway's

$\mathcal{F}$ our years ago I took the test and started a new career as a trained telephone worker at the King County Crisis Clinic in Seattle.

I saw an advertisement calling for volunteers to help shoulder the heavy workload at the local clinic. A few days went by until I made the call, and within a week I found the clinic's invitation in my mailbox.

$\mathcal{T}$ he first get-acquainted-meet would start that coming Wednesday at 7 PM. On my way, the traffic creeping over the I-90 Bridge crossing Lake Washington had come to a standstill. That's normal during the early evening hours. Why had I not thought of this? Why had I ignored the traffic to the baseball game at 8 PM that helped freeze all roads into elongated parking lots?

A little after seven I managed to get a call in to the clinic. I would be late, actually rather late.

"Should I still show up?"

"Yes, Claus, come on in. You cannot turn around to go home anyway. We allow our phone workers one late show per year. You just had yours. See you soon."

I do not like to be late for anything and for sure not for this first meeting. What kind of a volunteer will this guy turn out to be? I am certain somebody had this question come to mind. I felt apologetic, in the minus column, even before I got there.

This Crisis Clinic represented for me a new beginning. Retired by then, I had healed from cancer surgery and distanced myself from the ever-present fear of what might happen to me next.

All through my professional career I had been responsible for large numbers of people. I directed the engineering and managed the manufacture of heavy sea-going machinery.

Contribute — this word, a meaningful reminder to be counted on, cast in polished bronze on my desk, greeted employees and visitors.

And one day after my recovery from cancer surgery I met with myself and discovered I still knew how to spell that word. A television advertisement —

"…we … Clinic …"

—poked me.

The door to the conference room stood wide open. More than twenty minutes late, hesitant, I entered. The thirty or so people turned around and clapped. The speaker in front waved for me to take a seat among women and men, younger and older.

Though a little unsure of myself, a feeling rose in me that I had done right to apply. Still, I worried whether they would accept a recovering alcoholic.

The speaker picked up where my entrance had interrupted her.

"Welcome. I am Martha Dugon, training supervisor. Your name, who you are, and why you are here, tell us, please."

I stood up and turned to the crowd.

"I am Claus Hackenberger…"

My wife and I and our four-year-old son had emigrated from Germany in 1956. I talked about my career in engineering and told them, except for living ten years in Alaska, home had always been around this Puget Sound country. How old? I did not say, but I shared I am a recovering alcoholic and want to help…

The gang clapped again. Why they did makes no difference. Their welcome made me feel good.

"All right, then. I am just telling these wonderful people here that the supervisor in the phone room will always have the last word. You might be asked to say something to the caller you don't like, you might be asked to end the call while you think you have not said all the things you had in mind, but we ask you to go by what they suggest. The supervisor has done this work for many years and has gathered a lot of experience to assist you. Both supervisors may listen in on your discussion with the caller. This will help you to never feel alone during any of the calls."

Some time later, after a few shifts under my belt, I ran into one of the situations Ms. Martha Dugon had trained us for.

"Hang up, Claus. Tell her you are ending the call."

"Claus, listen—end the call!"

"Claus?"

It is very hard to end a call when the young woman crying tells you she has failed the state's recovery system three times. The only place left for her remained the street, an emergency room at a hospital, and possibly jail.

"Karen, I have other calls waiting, I need to—"
"Oh, go to hell, you fucking son of a bitch!"
Click!
My face twitched.

*A*ll permanent supervisors at the clinic possess a master's degree in one of the many health sciences.

That first evening, all of us got to work answering the screening questionnaire. I do not think it proper to spell out what we were asked, but I can assure you it projected the strong backbone of this all-important organization. Its professionalism down to the dot at the end of a sentence keeps this Crisis Clinic on par with the reality of every new day's life.

Nearly a week went by. They didn't take me? Why not? I came up with all kinds of valid reasons that broke my confidence into big chunks. Then, finally Thursday evening my phone rang.

"Hello, are you Claus? Oh, good. I am Judy, the mother of all our volunteers at this here place on Mercury Street. I want to ask if you could come by tomorrow morning to discuss your answers."

My gears were spinning. I am a recovering alcoholic. What else could it have been? I went over and over the questionnaire. I had given my truthful answers to those sticky questions on birth control, yeah, and God. But she did not mention any of those specifics while we were talking on the phone.

I got there at nine, on time, worth mentioning.

"You see, Claus, the person calling somehow or other wants help, knowingly or not. Your answer to this person is immensely important, and the way you deliver your sentences, believe me, every word weighs heavily. You, like all the other phone workers, will hear from drunks, from drug addicts, talk to the lost and not found homeless people. Rich or poor, you might bear witness to someone shooting himself while you are talking to that person. During training we will give you tools to handle this onrush of misery.

"We do not want you to personalize the calls unless your supervisor allows you to. Opinions about God and how you feel about an unborn fetus should stay with you. Do you follow me?"

"Yes, I do."

"But like always, there will be exceptions, and you will get acquainted with these during the coming weeks. Tell me, can you live with that?"

"No need to worry. I understand why it has to be that way."

"Well, then…"

She got up from her chair,

"Congratulations, Claus. I welcome you to our training class. Here, take your binder. My door stays always open. Good to have you with us. Sometime soon, I would like to hear more about the book you are writing."

A little shaky but very contented, I walked back to the elevator.

Ms. Dugon, "our trainer," turned out to be one of the best teachers I ever had the privilege to listen to. Think "tough." The three hours of training every night for six weeks were filled with how to listen, to speak, how to be an efficient phone worker. Some of my coworkers went to work each day. Some were foster parents. I had it easy, the in-service, retired Claus. Easy? None of these phone calls, I would learn, would be "easy."

Before long, these women and men whom I sat beside at the clinic became a new and important part of my family. Often their urge to help others grew from their own pain. For myself, I tried to make amends for the many bad situations I had caused during my years. To whom I made those amends bore no importance. I did it for the many in this world I hurt, whether they are still alive or have died or I cannot reach.

I needed heroes to look up to. Well, this Crisis Clinic grew heroes who fought for those who had given up, for those who no longer knew under which bridge they might rest that night.

Yes, the people at the Clinic were and always will be my heroes—women and men who taught me to be humble, to see the real day and how this day lives at the other side of the fence.

*E*very call carried its special signature. Often hard words came over the line. I heard the tears being wept, listened to the slurring of the alcoholic responses. The issues callers cried into our ears were immense and overwhelmingly complex. Loneliness, illness, violence, young or old, women and men totally without hope, being abused, drunk, hooked on drugs, hungry...

"I don't want to live anymore..."

I figured I'd been down the alley a few times, around some blocks. I would be prepared, would have the right answers.

How much I did not know!

I had not the faintest clue of how far and how long a person can walk without seeing the light of the day. The hours in the phone room were counted in high-intensity minutes and none short of sixty. Aware not to get personally involved, I had a difficult time with this instruction. I often fell into the trap that I must and right now fix the caller's problem. It took time for me to realize I only could vouch for her or his safety as long as we kept talking.

I should have known I could not change a person's habit in five minutes more or less, could not, in fact, ever make that person change. I only—maybe—could be of help. So, why all of a sudden was I so affected by my inability to right what was wrong? The severe hopelessness from which some people reached out to us spoke so loud, laden with pain, felt to me so immensely devastating. This kept hurting me over and over. God, I must be able to change that situation right now, at that moment. It hit me unmercifully and especially when I talked with young adults.

After about a year, I changed my shift from Monday afternoon to Wednesday morning. My new supervisor, Joey, had worked at the clinic for over twenty years. Her reservoir of knowledge and hands-on experience showed no horizon. She passed on to me the other side of the coin, a less strict system and a wide tolerance for feelings. Compassion and goodness percolated from her into discussions we had regarding life and love, forgiveness, coping, taking care of oneself—all kinds of subjects. Joey, our reward, our gift. She and I became good friends.

She acted as my personal film critic.

"Hey, Claus, you can endure a little violence. No way can you miss this one."

She often had a list of videos for me to rent.

In the three years I served as a trained volunteer phone worker, I spent 1,480 hours, at least one five-hour shift per week and often two, the declared limit. The time fulfilled me, gave back to me a sense of belonging and the confidence that I still can help.

Some days had happy endings. Many others did not. Suicide calls penetrated all of my defenses.

The ongoing conversations in the phone room are considered as highly confidential. What happened there stayed there. I do not think I am violating this basic rule when I talk of one call I am trying to but cannot forget.

I had started at seven in the morning. Judging by the number of calls coming in that early, I guessed this shift would turn busy. It did. The four of us worked hard to get to all the calls.

Halfway into the shift, a short pause let Kelly, working across from me, tell a joke. I never heard the punch line. My phone rang.

"Hi, Crisis Clinic, Claus here. May I help you?"

A German-speaking man asked if I would talk to him. He knew only a little English.

"Ja, talk to me. I am here for you. By what name may I call you?"

"I, Bernhard. Done. No more like life. I am kill me…"

"Bernhard, could you and I talk about that? Can you tell me why you want to do that?"

Suicide calls instantly get the attention of the supervisor. Immediately did I raise my hand to signal my emergency. Joey came to sit next to me. She would help me with this call. Believe me, I needed her assurance. With her at my side, a tremendous relief swept over me.

Bernhard kept talking to me in German mixed with English. He stood on a stool in the basement. He had a rope wound around his neck with the other end tightly fastened to a cross girder above him. I had to get him to tell me what he thought right then at that moment. That is the first job of the phone worker on such a call—to ask specific questions to assemble a "suicide assessment."

"Why do you want to end your life? Have you tried to end your life before?"

His grief turned into deep, soul-ripping sobs.

"Claus, wife slept with other man. She, my son all I have in world here…"

His weeping tore into me. Joey put her hand on my arm and motioned for me to listen and to allow for quiet moments.

"Bernhard, there might be another way, so you do not need to take your life. Ja?"

He did not answer for a few minutes. I heard him breathe heavily. Joey nodded.

"Bernard, for how long have you been planning to end your life?"

He had tried sleeping pills a couple of weeks ago, but his son accidentally walked in on him in the bathroom. He did not take the rest of the pills, but dropped them into the sink. He could not go to work the next morning.

"Bernhard, we can keep talking, yes? Let's be safe, okay? I would like you to take the rope from your neck, please. Do you feel you can do that? Can you take it off, please? "

"No! No, no! Werner school soon. I must go now."

"Werner, that's your son? How old?"

"Twelve. He good boy in school. I love him, I...I do love him."

A burst of tears led to an extended coughing spell.

We talked about his son with spacious silence in between sentences. I needed to somehow come to the point where I could be reasonably sure that he would be out of immediate danger.

I knew what I said next could make or break him. I looked at Joey. I remembered time back, when I worried about saying the "right words" when answering the caller. She had said to me then,

"Claus, you care, you always will say the right words."

I now took my strength from that assurance.

"Okay, Bernhard, beautiful, so good that you love him. And I am sure he also loves you, right?"

He did not say anything for a while. I heard him crying, talking to himself of forgiving, of Werner, of Clara, most likely his wife.

Joey's eyes encouraged me to go on.

"Bernhard, what would Werner feel coming home from school and see you hanging in the basement?"

Silence and silence.

I heard a terrible noise, that of a chair scraping over the concrete floor. Oh my God! I stared at Joey.

And then!

"Claus! Claus!" Bernhard shouted. "No rope, off. Claus, I sit on chair. You are… You are right. Vielen Dank, Danke schoen, oh mein Gott… Thank you, Claus…"

I interrupted him.

"Bernhard, you feel calmer, yes? You feel safe? I am so very happy. Hey, Bernhard, I ask you, please, to see a doctor right away…yes, right now. Will you allow me to get help to get you to the hospital? It might be a police officer and an ambulance..."

"The police? No, no, I do no wronk..."

I took time to explain why the police will have to come to his home. They would help him to be safe on his way to the hospital. He finally agreed he would wait, gave me his address and phone number.

I kept him talking, asking him from where in Germany he had come from, telling him that I was from Heidelberg.

He had calmed down—a sob here and there, but no more crying. My God, thank you.

Our assistant supervisor contacted the police. What a relief to hear the officer knocking at Bernard's door, the strong, calm voice confirming their presence.

It had taken forty minutes, my longest call ever.

Joey took me to a room adjacent to the phone room. She gave me a long hug and then sat still until my hands no longer shivered.

"Well done, Claus. For the moment he is safe. Remember we cannot change lives. We have only options to offer. You want to go home, it's all right. Do something you like, be good to yourself."

I decided to stay. It would not have been fair to my friends in the phone room. We were busy. I had to fill out a lengthy, detailed report plus other paperwork for the clinic

I eventually left the team because my answers, my suggestions, my advice for the callers were turning hollow, without my heart in what I said. The many people at the end of their road were worth more than I could continue to give. I felt it was time to move on.

It had been a difficult task to take on—and perhaps even more difficult to leave.

*A*rriving home from my last shift at the Crisis Clinic in Seattle I did not know what to do with myself. My mind hung with my friends who just had hugged me good-bye. I missed that family already. I felt sad, suddenly not so sure whether I had been right leaving them behind.

It rained pretty hard, as if to dilute the uncertainty rising inside me.

My mailbox at the Renton Highland Post Office showed empty; not even a piece of junk mail greeted me.

I left my car parked at the post office and walked across NE 4th Street we in Renton call "Cemetery Road." What else could come by to help my sad mood grow sadder?

I lifted my sight off the pavement and saw the wind tearing at the flapping banner attached to the columns of *my* newly remodeled Safeway store.

Grand Opening
Come in and see

What a deal! Lowest prices, guaranteed. The store buzzed with customers, clerks, and well-dressed top management from out of town. The way they looked reminded me of the IBM sales and service crews during the sixties and early seventies: black suit, white shirt, and black tie.

The past sometimes will not leave me alone.

I do not like to shop when I am hungry. I had skipped lunch, felt not much like eating. But it did not stop me melting for the ice cream ad: "*Buy one, get one free.*" I filled the cart with things I didn't even know existed. Am I nuts? My refrigerator, not big enough, could not keep all this stuff cool. I would have to give one ice cream drum to my neighbor, who would no doubt accuse me of trying to fatten him up—but accept it anyway.

The overhead speakers playing "You Are My Sunshine" got steadily interrupted by loud announcements.

At the bakery the ladies have cookies for the little ones… Please, visit our new wine rack arrangement… Use your Safeway Club Card…yada. yada, yada…

The checkouts were humming. All reminded me of ants that just could not remember how to get back to their hill. I felt tempted to park my cart, leave it, and walk away. All the stuff I bought, only half will I use.

Embedded in the shortest checkout line, I noticed young, beautiful Nance waving at me over from behind the Video/Lotto stand where she worked. I usually buy from her those infamous "Sorry, you are not a winner" tickets. I figured she wanted to talk and wedged myself through the masses. She rushed at me, her face aglow with happiness and excitement.

"Claus, I am pregnant! I just found out from the doctor. My husband and daughter, they will be so very happy. But you know before them, Claus! I could not reach them, so I told you instead."

We hugged.

"Wow, Nance, that's beautiful, really beautiful. Thank you for sharing your news with me."

All I could bring forth. In the midst of this tumultuous crowd of customers, checkers, VIPs, and low prices, I lived a shining star moment. This woman touched me with a new life becoming in her. It pointed my heart in a different direction. I felt no longer sadness but loud joy.

Peace embraced this moment.

When Nance gave birth, I drew up a few lines to share their happiness:

Claus Hackenberger

people   people   people

north and south and east and west

did you hear?
just up the street
a prince, they say

not royalty
just a boy

a prince, yes
I know, born just
the other day

a prince
in that little house?
what's his name?

Andreas Chase

that does sound like royalty
so let's not wait around
write down good wishes
build heavenly dreams for him

new life
so beautiful

all right
let us congratulate
bring flowers for his family
sing and holler and dance and
turn the night into happy days

Life

Citizens!

Awake.

*My dawn came to light
prepared for the birth of a timeless sunrise.*

*I want to greet you, my friends,
and share this moment.*

*A bee, deeply humming,
zigzagged through my room.
A hard "clack," an ensuing silence…
these opposing events spurred me
to search for the intruder.*

It did not take long.

*On her back,
legs frantically clawing for help,
she would not give up.*

In my younger years,
ailing with MMS (Male Macho Syndrome),
I squeezed such creatures
– stinging daughters of bitches –
flatter than 20-weight laser paper.
I had to protect my children
from the pain and disease these carriers dispensed.

Or so I told myself...

Now, fifty years later,

I lent the little creature my left index finger
then carried her outside.
She buzzed into the scented morning breeze.
I waved a wish:

Bee, live and fly.

Greetings, Claus

Forgive Me

Year 2007. I am eighty.
Today, war, the media's most familiar word, has screaming women bend over their mangled husbands. Fear grows round the globe, everywhere. Missiles scorch the sky. Exploding targets strobe into our living room. Real blood reddens sidewalks at many cities, ours and "theirs." Do our eyes still see this?
We keep hearing our leaders tell us

>...there is no other way...

Do maimed minds, torn-apart people arbitrate dispute? Do children squatting next to their parents covered with tarps assure both their and our new and better tomorrows?

Year 1943. I am 16.
We keep hearing our leaders tell us

...there is no other way...

But World War II.
Hitler.

I lived through those nights, firestorms braising city after city, killed and killed and killed.

Year 1998. I am 71.
At the municipal offices in my town, I applied for a utility hookup at the cozy house I just had bought.
Eloise came running.
Greetings, Claus, greetings!
My work over the years cleaning up a large superfund site had allowed us to become good friends. Broken supply lines caused extreme water bills. Eloise, utility department chief, and I negotiated on an ongoing basis. Besides being well versed in these matters, Eloise also filled her day with a warm understanding of people.
Hey, Claus, you look good. How've you been?
We talked, memories bubbled over, slid back and forth over the countertop.
By the way, we have a new volunteer at the desk. She came from England.
Eloise performed the introduction.
Versie, Claus here knows this place inside out. A few years back he came to visit us here nearly every day.

*N*ot very tall, fragile, snow-white hair, about my age. Her eyes searched my face as she reached for my hand. I offered both of mine. The fingers on her right hand were crippled.

"The Germans gave this to me. Look at my nose. See the line where my lips had been cut by flying glass? One of your V-1s hit our house near London. The dent in my head here…"

She turned sideways.

"…from shrapnel, same with my hand, a few days after my seventeenth birthday. How old were you?"

"Seventeen. At that time I'd been a gunner…"

*G*od, where are you? Did I just say that? No, someone else must have spoken that sentence.

More than fifty years ago "my" V-1 hit her house. I still know the sound of those explosions. Oh, Lady, forgive me, please, let me undo my words! I, the German V-1 man, tells you he had been the gunner. Lord, I should lose my voice for that.

"You look worried. Claus, I'm not angry anymore. No, I'm not angry at you. Please, believe me."

She smiled with hidden pain, pain that never would go silent.

Eloise started the clock again. Cheerfully, as always, she beckoned.

Hey, man, come on, we need to sign you up. Without the paperwork you are not going to have heat or light tonight.

"Versie, I'll be back."

When I returned from filling out the never-ending forms, Versie told me she goes to see a psychiatrist every two weeks. She cannot forget the screams, the thundering noise of her house splintering, the pressure of the detonation, her bleeding face. We had talked for a while when she looked at me.

"Now, let us be friends, yes? We need to be friends. The Lord, you know, taught us to forgive…"

We hugged for a long while.

"Yes, friends."

And then I ran out to my car and I cried.

Versie, I will pray for you every morning. Whenever I pass by, I will wave my hello to you. I will bring you flowers. Yes, and I'll paint a scene for you, and when I bring it we'll talk of sunshine, spring, rainbows, rivers, the ocean, good things you can hold in your heart.

Yes! Yes, I'll do that! I cannot undo the past, our past, but I will try to brighten our future.

She inhaled the heady scent from my garden's flowers. She kept the painted picture by her desk. Whenever I came by to pay my bill, we talked of both ordinary life and intimate longings.

One day she brought for me three green frogs with funny faces and magnets in their bellies. Her small white cross "I LOVE JESUS" continues to decorate my fridge and my home. The frogs hold "important" scribbles on paper slips telling me not only of tomorrow's chores, but also what I missed to do yesterday.

And the leaders of nations keep telling us…

...there is no other way...

but war, but killing, but torture, but tearing the fabric of our being, but deceiving, but spending the life of humankind irresponsibly and without accountability.

Time

Behind the walls, the days melted one into another. How to make time once again mean something to me?

Inspiration came in the form of a discarded, gray-green hash can. With the help of a stolen pair of pliers, I cut and bent and twisted the thing into a pot with two handles. I carried water in it to wash my face. I slurped potato peel soup from it at dinner time.

In one of my many walks around the barbed area of the tent city, I found a rock with a sharp edge. I used this every day to inscribe a short scratch on the side of my pot.

With these simple tools, I invited time back into my life.

Eventually the handles rusted away from the can, and I had to let go of this calendar of mine. I counted 563 scratches before I dumped the pot with the rubble at the quarry they worked me at.

Each short mark around the outside of that hash can represented one full day in slavery.

Ever since, time has fascinated me. I have spent uncounted hours asking myself unanswerable questions.

When did time begin?
Without man, would time exist?
Does time in fact exist at all?
Are time and God the same?
Could life regenerate itself in the absence of time?

After returning home from imprisonment, I wrote poems asking time about its cruelty, about the inconsistency with which it fit both long and short moments in identical spans. Over the years I never ceased asking questions, even though I knew answers would not, could not be forthcoming.

I failed miserably again and again in getting acquainted with the essential relationship between yesterday and tomorrow, now and eternity. When I wrote a chapter about time for my nascent book, I fell short once again in cracking its code.

And so, time will forever be defined best for me by 563 crude scratches etched on the side of an old tin can.

Perhaps that is the simplest, truest explanation of time we can ever know.

Code 4

Days and horrible nights had come and gone without my being aware of my whereabouts. Disembodied faces grinning at me, the horse and buggies traveling on the road upside down, the children wearing strangely oversized heads walked on one leg only while they carried the other leg slung over their shoulder like a shawl—these frightened me. Dogs, too, stood upright, smoking cigarettes, talking to an assembly of black-coated nurses that dragged curled-up plastic tubing behind them. Faces raced by, a grossly distorted kaleidoscope in psychedelic colors.

This scenery came to life every time I closed my eyes. I tried to keep them open, but that did not work.

Another time I sat in front of a switchboard pretending I knew how to do the switching. The thousand or so tiny levers jabbered, demanding to be flipped. I panicked, gasping for the air someone seemed to have shut off.

A steady clicking noise, like the primitive language of a valve, wanted to assure me air kept rushing into my lungs. Still, I saw me close to death, and at one moment I wanted to stop living despite the inrushing air trying to save me.

The switchboard expanded to an enormous size. All switches disappeared except for one—big and red and way up high where I could not reach. Somebody had built a glass fence around this switch. Like grimly determined cheerleaders, the one-legged children danced inside the fence. A giant man came walking down the narrow street lined with cardboard house fronts. His whole body, except for the head, was wrapped in black sack cloth.

If I wanted to stop living, the man said, I needed to flip that unreachable lever. Ugly, I still can see his skinless face, the crooked teeth penetrating through his cheeks.

"Go, flip that switch, hurry, come on, you can stretch that far. Hey, reach just a little higher. I will ask the kids to trample down that stupid fence."

I tried so hard. The pain in my chest turned unbearable...

Recalling, rethinking the events happening after my surgery, I come to see how these hallucinations tricked my internal systems. Why would I have wanted to die when all my prayers before begged to get through this alive?

Fumbling for this switch also happened earlier in my life, and more than once. In those incidences the switch was well in sight. I did touch the lever to get to the end. There were no unbearable chest pains holding me back when I walked the Narrows Bridge in Tacoma in a storm-torn night. No one pushed me to proceed with my planned jump. But neither did I hear the voice asking me not to.

Time back in war prison camps, with a minimum chance of survival, I did not even think of taking my life. During those three years I discovered an uttermost will in me to keep living.

Later, during my work at the Seattle Crisis Clinic, I listened to men, women, and young folks screaming for hope to soothe their desperation. I talked to people on the phone while they prepared to hang themselves from the rafters in the basement.

Remembering those phone calls, I come away convinced I never could take my life. I cannot see any reason for doing so. I live now, but I also believe and expect my tomorrow.

A voice penetrated. I felt somebody touching my arm. "…wake…your eyes…squeeze my hand… Claus! Claus!"

A woman smiled at me. She held my hand with both of hers.

"Claus, soon you will feel better. I am your nurse today. You can call me Victoria. I will help you to get well. We will do this together. Deal?"

"What's happening? Am I… Where…?"

After open heart surgery, I had been brought to the Intensive Care Unit on the fifth floor at Jason Memorial Hospital.

"Your children are waiting to see you. You think you want to invite them in?"

Yes, they were standing outside the room, waving behind the glass door. Seemed my nodding opened that door. I got a lot of kisses, though Misha and Peter wore worried faces. My daughter Christine cried. They read to me from the green board on the wall near the entrance. The nurses updated it daily:

Today is Monday the 28th of March, 2004.
Victoria is your nurse for this day

The children added their get well wishes, drew a flower and smiley faces. I must have drifted away, for when I looked around for them, they had gone.

Hour by hour, my world became more real. Victoria changed a few wires connected to my chest. She refurbished the "Bag-Tree" with fresh plastic bags and adjusted the drip clamp on one or two.

"Claus, take this and press it down onto your chest." She handed me a large stuffed, bright-red heart, someone's idea of a visual pun. "You need to cough so your lungs clear up. You will hurt, but the pillow will lessen that pain. Try, I'll wait."

She put her hand on my forehead while I dared to cough. Yes, pain, terrible pain screamed from my wounded chest. But by evening I no longer needed to dare. My body made the effort for me, coughing endlessly from bad congestion.

Victoria finished her shift. A young man, Angelo, the night shift nurse, brought a small paper cup half filled with a greenish, toothpaste-flavored liquid.

"Here, Claus, drink up, please. This medicine will make you sleep and help to quiet your cough."

He sat down at the rim of the bed and talked to me. Not that I remember what we spoke about, still his low, compassionate voice resides in my memory.

Angelo became my friend as Victoria did, and Sean, who had prepared me for the surgery. Sean has a gift he shares with his patients, an unadulterated kindness and warmth. Anxious, frightened, I tried to out-guess tomorrow. What if I don't make it? What if I don't heal right? What if I end up in a wheelchair? Sean understood my fear. He took my hand and held on to me. I breathed easier.

Early one morning, a physical therapist arrived, a short fellow, crew-cut, no-nonsense, introduced himself as my personal trainer. I endured his rehearsed, five minute speech he rattled off without taking a breath.

"Sir, you must start walking. Your heart…"

After a while, Eemha, "my" dayshift nurse, and Garth, the trainer, helped me to sit up and then slid me down from the mattress. I remember feeling weightless.

"Come on, we'll walk once around the nurses' center, okay?"

The care unit is circular, like a wheel, with the nurses' station being the hub and the six rooms laid around like spokes.

"Come, come, we'll try. You will be fine…"

Whether I wanted to or not, we took the stroll. Eemha preserved my dignity by tying the strings in the back of my hospital-issue nightie. The chromed bag-tree followed along like a dutiful pet. Nurses at the station hollered their hushed encouragement at our parade of three. We did one round; my legs told me not to do more.

*D*espite my being not quite "all there," I noticed Garth's tennie runners. If he would have tried to donate them in one of those clothes and shoe hampers at a grocery parking lot, the red Salvation Army dumpster would have burped them right back at him. Their disrepair sent me back to WWII and my time spent in French slave labor camps, where I did not have any shoes at all. We walked to and from the quarry on wooden soles held in place by canvas strips. Garth, your shoes at that time would have sold for a hundred bucks a side.

*A*fter the walk, the crew-cut sat in my room at the small table by the window and wrote his report. His brutal jabs of the pen abused the clipboard. Tiny pearls of sweat gathered at his forehead. He wiped his face with his forearm while holding his paperwork and pencil in that same hand. He promised to be back in the afternoon. All about him, the commanding posture reminded me of Napoleon.

Having written this, I now feel ashamed I did not like him at the time. The shape I happened to be in really cannot count as an excuse. He did his job as specified in the training manual, the physical rehab bible.

Why did I have to be so judgmental? Garth was fit, healthy, while I barely kept from falling off the cliff. I knew without exercise I would never get well, and he moved me through that tunnel. Waves still reverberate sometimes in me of an ugly arrogance I hosted during my booming years. I am sorry, Garth, I really am! Should you read these lines, please, forgive me. I have a hard time with being told. I respond better when asked.

Dr. V. stopped by.

"Mister Hackenberger, I am hearing you do not want to eat… No, please relax. Here is my proposal. This is your third day after we fixed you up. Tonight we will bring you our regular dinner. ICUs have good food. Should you, however, not take a bite, I will send my assistant with the order to force a tube down your throat."

His eyebrows rose, not quite a question.

"Yes, Dr. V., I understand."

"Good, you are doing better by the day. I like that. Thank you."

"I must thank you, sir. Your people here are so kind, so warm, so helping. I do feel good in your care. Ironic, I have to come near death to discover the immeasurable dedication of the people here at this unit…"

"Let them know."

Special souls must live with those who help torn human beings to heal. Day and night these nurses give all they have to share. They live with the illness and wounds of their patients. Hope rays from their faces. When they talked to me, helped me to sit upright in my bed, watched me swallow my medicine, when the night nurse pulled up the blanket and tucked me in—I felt safe and warm and at peace.

What could I do more than to say thank you? Those two words can never do, will never be enough. Those people gave me a gift, fragrant flowers I should not ever let go dry. I cannot do much anymore, but can help people to smile, even to laugh.

Before they let me go home I promised the whole nursing staff I would write about the time they cared for me and made me well.

*D*r. V. had performed the surgery on my heart. I learned after they peered at my insides that my heart muscle had been damaged much more than the tests had indicated. I know he saved my life, and I am so very much obliged to him.

I persuaded Eemha to divert Napoleon's afternoon visit and promised I would eat my dinner that evening. She and her nurse's helper half-carried me over to the small table by the window, sat me down, and wrapped me in a warm blanket. I looked out and saw no smoking dogs nor horses galloping upside down, but real people going about their evening.

The food came, and while I did not eat all of it, the wonderful night nurse nodded her approval.

The coughing gradually became less severe. But my red heart cushion suffered from FPS—frequent pressure syndrome.

Days went by. I had the opportunity to talk with "my" nurses who constantly and instantly took care of me. I had been brought into a new family of uttermost dedicated women and men, a marvelous gang of human beings.

Eemha had been born in India. Her parents moved their family to Uganda, from where she traveled to England. She found her man at med school while she entered the surgical nursing field. This tall, tender woman came in on her day off to show me her three-year-old son. Her husband worked at a different hospital in town.

"Eemha, what made you decide to care for broken people? Where do you take your strength from?"

"I grew up in countries amidst pour and ill people. Whenever my will falters I think of the towns I came from. Life is rough there at best..."

Like the other nurses, she brought joy and hope to me while I struggled to breathe without the help of oxygen.

*M*arcia cheered into my room and announced, "Come on, Claus, we will give you a bath. Not that you smell bad, but we want to relax you..."

I laughed, pressing the red, larger-than-life heart cushion into my chest.

The night after the bath, I did not find my sleep button. Joshie, the night nurse, helped me to the table by the window. She wrapped me in blankets, freshly baked in the warming oven.

The street way down looked forlorn, the rain fell on only a few people hurrying about. The hospital slept but the nurses kept watch.

I heard the radio's low voice entering the ICU.

C O D E 4 - seven minutes.

A short time after this announcement I saw the ambulance strobes heading toward what I guessed would be the emergency room. The station bristled to life. Several nurses prepared the empty room next to mine, but this time they did not bring anybody to rest there.

Yet other calls from ambulances interrupted the silence. *C O D E 4, four minutes.*

Code 4—Code 4—Code 4. The next morning, we had no vacancies—all sold out.

Ever since, these two words hang with me. *Code 4,* 24/7, year after year, our nurses and doctors make us survive, and not only at this hospital but in one form or another all over our planet.

On Day 6, I woke up late. The early-morning shift had already taken all my "vitals." Cold scrambled eggs drifted by my nose, waiting to be ingested.

The chromed bag-tree had disappeared, two plastic tubes had been pulled out of my chest, and two injection ports had been bandaged. Where had I been when all this happened?

My daily walks around the circle became routine. Here and there I met one or two other walker-pushers. Nobody said much—there was nothing to say. Once in a while I had a chance to greet a patient through the open door of the room. But that did not happen every day. We all enjoyed privacy—OK with me.

"Well. Look at you, so much better! Everything must be going your way. Fantastic!"

"Good morning, Victoria, glad you are back. I missed you."

"…took off a few days. I registered with the Army to go to Iraq and help out there for a few months."

Did I hear right? She had a family, two sweet children and a caring husband.

"Oh?"

"Those broken soldiers need me more than the people I am helping here. Claus, you've been there. You told me in your book. There are not enough men and women around who could make up for those being blasted to pieces. I've got to do this. We'll celebrate when I get back!"

Though I was not allowed yet to get up by myself, I swung my legs out of the bed and hugged her for a long time. She would leave before Christmas.

Some afternoons I had visitors. Friends came by for a short take of my situation. The children had to drive for an hour and a half from Christine's house north of Seattle. During those visits we talked about the "new Claus." How would his life change, what would be in store for him? All who stopped by encouraged me and wished good health to be my partner.

I have to admit I worried about my future. Next year I would see eighty—how much time would there be left for me? Would I be able to take care of myself, be able to keep writing, to think straight, not to be a burden? Yes, I did worry about this "new Claus."

"My" cardiologist, Dr. G. came to check me over. He listened to this heart of mine such a long time. Does the new valve click right? Why does he have to listen so long to its beat?

"Claus, we let you leave here in a couple of days."

"To go home?"

"Not yet. To a rehab center close by where your daughter lives. The doctor there probably will keep you for another two weeks before you can join your family. I'll keep you posted. Good luck!"

Real news! No one had mentioned the words "Rehab Center." What for? I would find out soon.

Victoria saw my scared face, sat on my bed and explained.

"You need special care, need to learn to walk again, dress yourself. You also must have instant access to professional help…"

Her words did not let me worry less about this Rehab Center.

I pulled the big, red, cough-suppressant heart from under my blanket and begged her to take it with her. I had written a thank you note on the fabric, letting her know she would always have a spot in my new and improved heart. She took the cushion and gave me a kiss.

Later, after she made her way to that desert on the other side of the world, we stayed in touch by e-mail. The time she spent in those surgical tents must have been extremely painful, hard beyond description. I looked forward to talking with her face-to-face, hearing her words about what she had seen.

The homecoming celebration did not happen. We lost sight of one another.

Victoria, where are you?

*T*he day before rehab time, Angelo came by.

"I am not working today, but I wanted to tell you all of us feel we have known you before, have known you for a long time. You have helped us to care. Claus, should you ever need one of us, you come, and we will work things out."

His words touched me so, tears filled my eyes. Angelo took me in his arms.

"You will make a new day for yourself. Okay!"

He waved as he left. He has become a part of me.

*P*eter, my youngest son, had to go back to work managing the Alaska Railroad Yard in Anchorage. He hurried by for a hug and my thanks before flying home. On his way out he wrote on that green blackboard: *GO Vats GO.* That's German. The three words mean, *Come father, come. On with life!*

*D*eparture day.
The nurses on the shift dealt out lots of hugs. Christine and Eemha picked me up from the wheelchair and kind of slid me into the car. We arrived at the Rehab Center just before dark. A nurse wheeled me to the room I learned to call my home for nearly three weeks.

With her new baby to tend to, Christine said a quick goodbye. After she had left, I sat on that bed and felt the train coming, a train laden with uncertainty and fear. My roommate talked in his sleep. A curtain made two small stalls out of one. We could not see each other being in bed.

The night nurse, Brenda, brought the medicine and an oxygen generator. She adjusted the plastic tube so the little outlets fit right into my nose. The barometer, I remember read 3. I inhaled the "fresh air" deeply and simmered down a little.

"Lie down now. Here is the call button if you need anything. Good night."

God, I am so alone!

*U*nexpectedly the curtain at the end of the bed lifted and, like an angel, Allen, Christine's husband, appeared.

"Allen, it's so late, you—"

"Not to worry. Christine came home crying, hating to leave you all by yourself. I just wanted to say good night. We will be back in the morning. You have your cell phone, call us. Now sleep."

*T*he next morning… The next mornings…
Napoleon's "sister" arrived, pushed the curtain aside sharp at 8 AM. Even with my pain-tinted eyes I could see her beauty. Tall, very warmly she smiled, winning me at the first moment. Female Napoleons are easier to take than the crew-cut ones. I liked her.

"How did the night go for you, Claus?"

"I thought daylight never would come."

"Well, every night will be better. I am Ursula, but they call me Oola. You and I will work on getting back your strength every morning and after your nap in the afternoon."

Oola also had a clipboard with some preprinted sheets clamped to it.

"*I* brought your clothes from the closet over there. See, here they are laid out. I would like you to dress yourself. No hurry, we have time."

"Why do you want to watch me getting dressed?"

"Don't worry. This will help me to tailor your exercise program. All right?"

*M*eanwhile my neighbor strolled by in his wheelchair and like a sergeant shouted a good morning in my direction.

I found myself not being quite capable to put on anything. The socks refused to let my feet enter. Oola handed me a "sock puller," an indescribable contraption. Much to my surprise, the gadget worked.

I used one hour and seventeen minutes to get dressed, including the ten minutes I took to put on my shirt correctly the second time.

"Would you like to sit in your wheelchair and meet the neighborhood? Or do you…"

I just fell back onto my bed.

But I made my days turn better all the time. My roommate, Arne, came through as one hell of a good man. He had fallen in his living room and broken his hip. Unable to reach the phone, he lay there for one night and the following day.

"The phone kept ringing, but nobody came to help me up. I hurt and then some."

His son finally came by to check on the telephone.

The doctors replaced his joint and sent him here for therapy. His trainer, a young, strong man, showed up early each morning to help him get dressed and take him through the ringer. Saturdays and Sundays they allowed him to sleep in.

The food they gave me tasted good. I asked for smaller portions, but the kitchen ignored that request. Stan, the medical head nurse, explained it had to do with insurance matters. But the staff took very good care of my needs.

People I met while "racing" the hallways in my chair mostly were rather ill. Many came here to live out their lives.

Christine with baby Henry and Cona, the dog, visited me often and always brought some surprise.

I practiced walking stairs and eventually even enjoyed the physical therapy. Strange, but true, I became sad when I for the last time shook hands with Arne.

Code 4 — nearly three years...

And I had to fight for every better day, sometimes for every better hour. The anti-depression pills did nothing for me. I came to realize again no medicine can do its assigned job unless I allow my body to accept the prescription.

I had learned this earlier when the doctors removed my cancerous prostate. Just thinking a medicine will work proves not to be enough. I have to want sternly to get better. The doctor, the medicine, and I, that tripod will steady my progress.

P.S. to all of you wonderful people at the Jason Memorial Hospital: I send my thanks, my sincere and warm greetings.

Sometimes at Night

...sometimes at night
    when I look up at
        all the stars in the sky
            I wonder how it began
                the sky   the stars   the sea...
                          "earthmakers"

Hello, Monique,

Last Sunday, Orchestra Seattle Chamber Singers gave a very beautiful, soul-revving concert, "earthmakers." Carol Sams, a local composer, created this all-exciting piece. Seldom has music made for such turmoil inside me. Overwhelming, up-heaving, and embracing, this rhythm opened me up deep and wide!

I closed my eyes and felt my arms could reach this majestic universe that keeps exploding into an ever-evading, never-ending emptiness.

Crescendos of tearing dissonances, ebbing, chattering, spiking high only to collapse into soft harmonies, touched my every fiber.
I longed for you to listen with me.

On my way home I climbed down from my high. Southward, Mount Rainer ghosted through the night's haze. I felt small, pondered why I know so little about what I am supposed to do while here on this earth.

God entered my thoughts. I have tried to fathom my relationship with Him, and our world within His universe. I have asked. I keep asking. My untrained mind occasionally finds some answers, yet they vary with how I ask the question. Seldom do I hear a clear yes or no. Maybe no answer can do away with the shadows I wake when I shine light behind the many boulders.

I called.
Monique, lady? Early, you must have left already for work. All right, tonight.

I like to listen to her voice on her answering machine…
"So sorry, I'm away…"

Sensuous, warm.
Monique and I are good friends, more than friends. We love each other in many beautiful ways. Quite some time has passed since we first met. Tall, elegant, light-brown hair gathered in a bun, well-dressed, she teaches history at Seattle University.

One evening, last week, I hauled a bucket of Chinese food home for dinner. A little hot, yes, but OK. The fortune cookie's paper strip said to me:

Pull the universe inside you. Make it your own.

While I rolled the innocent printing into a tiny ball, I wondered how I could own the universe. It seemed not possible.

Why?

See, I do not exactly know what the universe does. I cannot make something my own that I do not understand. Besides, I do not believe anyone can own the universe.

Days went by, yet this white, narrow strip of paper did not let go of me. God came to mind. I do not know Him well enough either to be His owner.

I've been taught to believe in God since I became able to understand my mother's words. I embraced Him during my childhood, despite the gruesome strings people have tacked onto His image. Should I ever lose my belief in Him, should I ever doubt Him, Hell would be all I could expect. Hell would become my next stay.

Who invented Hell, the anti-Heaven?

Why does man do that, coaching a Devil to be the antimatter to God?

Monique, you must know, I do have God! His grace does lead me. Nothing I accomplished during my time here on this earth could have been successfully processed without His forgiveness, and help.

"So what's the big deal?" you might ask. "What more do you want? What for are you digging?"
It's the way I am. If I cannot ask, cannot doubt and search, I cannot believe. And that goes for everything else along my way.

This God, I see Him different from what I have been taught. The word "God" to me sounds different, much mightier than I hear it said by my friends. This God has been made into a human, but for me He is not the fixer of all my problems. He does not have to micromanage his creation.

He offers Grace. I see Him as the one Father for all people—past, present, and for life in the future. Yes, He listens to different names at different places around our planet. How could that be a problem? Far East in Taiwan, I said a Hail Mary. I remember, my knees hurt on the cool jade floor in a temple that belonged to Buddha. I felt very close to God then.

Monique had voicemailed her questions.

"How can you believe in both God and Evolution? Could we discuss Darwin tonight?"

She came to my house that evening as the oncoming night cooled the day. She wore shorts and a light-blue tank top. She held her shiny hair in a filigreed silver broche. A narrow diamond bracelet glittered from her left wrist, my gift after our first hug.

I had readied myself for a serious discussion. Monique needed to know about my continuous bouncing between blasphemy and total surrender to a God I do not know.

I did not make my speech. I listened instead. She wanted me to drive us to the beach near Burien. Darwin and the Galapagos Islands occupied us during the half-hour drive.

> "Keep your eyes on the road. Later you can look at me."

We walked the beach and found a log to sit on. With her warm, dark eyes on me, she began with the voice of an angel,

> "Give your hands to me. Tell me you are well, you are at peace with yourself and God. Take my love I share with you. I want to help you find the answers you are longing for."

We sat into the night, listened to the lapping of the sea running on shore.

Evolution—I believe God himself wrote the agenda. With a few single cells He seeded life, gave them methane to breathe, embedded them in aboriginal slime deep under the ocean, and let them simmer into life as we know today. Why should I feel degraded, less human, accepting that?

"This God, your God, Claus, is a good God…"

I still hear my mother's voice and see her stern face while she warned me never to test Him.

But then, we keep killing life, His life. We tear it apart with most gruesome tools, with unthinkable hate. I wonder why He made us this way, why He allows man to be cruel?

Monique, forgive me, but during my drinking days I felt less than nothing for Him. Today, I shiver in my nakedness.

During sober moments, I thanked Him for having me be born at a place different from the ones where children grow up in bleeding clothes.

"It's not God who is doing that. It's the Devil…"

Time ago, a priest had said that to me before he gave me his absolution.

Is the Devil God's doing? Or did man help out again to keep up fear? But I did not dare to ask that question at the time.

I picked up Monique for a drive to Alki Beach west of Seattle. Beautiful! The office towers tinseled their lights while the setting sun poured liquid gold over the high-rises.

Monique, I love you.

What about the Soul? They say human beings own a God-given soul, living inside the body. A soul lives in me? What's my

soul made of? Does all life have one, not only humans? Littleman, my black poodle has a soul? I think he does.

> "Stay with me tonight. Your woman wants to fall asleep while you hold her..."

Monique, I feel odd. Do I, do I not believe in Him? Why do I dare Him?

She took my hand, pulled my arm around her, and let me listen to the beating of her heart.

When I switched the light off and pulled the blanket way high up under our chins, she whispered,

> "Daring Him? I think you dare us, we who thorn by thorn keep blurring what we have not understood from the outset on."

I dreamed of cathedrals, of beautiful music, paintings, and of poetry, all created with an insatiable urge to please Him.

I pray, I pray, yet I am missing that urge.

Why?

At the Beach

*M*y dog, Littleman, and I walk the beach nearly every day. We've been here when the rain fell in solid sheets, when angry waves thundered ashore, when gusts lifted seagulls to soar like kites. We have walked, too, amidst summer wavelets cooling both our feet and the gray sand even as the sun torched the land.

Storm tides shift the old driftwood up the sloped beach to make room for a new harvest of twisted trunks and sea-shaved logs. Some still carry their roots with them, which makes the intertwined mangle all the more grotesquely beautiful, powerful, enthralling.

We walk slowly, not many steps at a time. Littleman revisits his markers. I let my eyes travel beyond the horizon, caressing dreams of a bygone time when life in immeasurable abundance let me fill my days with treasures upon treasures. Paris, Venice, Bordeaux, Barcelona, Genoa, New York, Taipei, New Orleans, San Francisco…

Once in a while I sit down. Littleman rests in my lap. But this pose never lasts. His impatient stirring tells me we came here to walk, not to sit. I believe he could pee at those logs all day long.

To the right, far away, the island ferries cross the seaway. When the wind blows from the north I can hear the groan of their tooting horns.

Littleman hardly ever leaves much space between him and me, yet I scare when he disappears behind drifted detritus and I cannot see him. Sure, he feels safe in this seaside heaven; no need for me to whistle at him. Eventually, his head bobs up. His eyes dart in my direction and he zooms towards me. His ears usually hang down, rounding his teddy bear face. At his speed, though, these floppy lobes turn into a pair of stiff weather vanes. His whole body stretches into a streak scratched in the sand with a black permanent marker. I talk to him, pat this little friend of mine, and let him know how much I like him. I think he understands, but who can say? He chases off again, lured to his favorite smells.

I tire easily. We do a mile in about an hour or so. Returning to our starting line close to the road, I snap the leash back to his harness. He finds my car and waits for me to open the passenger door. I help him in, circle around the back of the Malibu, and then squeeze my frame between the steering wheel and driver's seat. Littleman greets me wildly, as though we haven't seen each other in weeks. While I fasten my seatbelt, release the brake, and start the motor, he sits on his hind legs. Cagily, he tilts his head a little, and with his shiny black eyes, forces me to unzip the plastic bag with his treats. He takes the bit from in between my fingers, ever so careful not to hurt me. He also wants water, even if he only takes one lick. I cannot help it, I have to give him a hug. After those ceremonies, I inch my car from our cramped parking space and hit the road.

On the way home he crawls on my lap and falls asleep. What a doggy day!

Darkness

*I thrust light
into the cave
waiting for me*

*daring darkness
shivers my fear*

*gargoyles
shriek at the flicker
from my lantern*

*spider's webbing
sticks to my face
ties my hands*

*my path slithers
hot wax
drowns the wick*

*dark turns black
shadows die
will I*

*quakes
fires
break the earth
and
beyond ashes
my broken life
finds heaven*

Leavenworth

One afternoon, a week before Christmas, I drove across Stevens Pass to the small Bavarian town of Leavenworth. I had been booked the following morning on KOHO, the local radio station, for an on-air interview. The host wanted to acquaint the listeners with my first book, A LONG WALK.

In the summer I would have gotten up at 5AM or so and pushed the gas pedal right through Blewett Pass. Two hours, tops.

Now, winter wrote a different script, surprised even our weathermen, frightened Sunday drivers, and lured noncombatants into ditches and snow berms.

I checked the pass reports. Heavy snow, high winds, freezing temperatures. While most Seattleites facing the west-to-east drive worried, I did not. I had lived ten years in Anchorage, Alaska, so for me the weather report outlined a stormy but normal winter day.

I decided to wing right through this mess, discarding troublesome thoughts about the other chauffeurs who might not realize I shared the same road. And I did see people unfamiliar with ice-slick pavements drive into one another, but I managed to escape any unfortunate meetings with my fellow travelers.

Even though I knew how to drive with skill and confidence on iced roads covered with snow, this afternoon would test my nerve. The higher up I got, white became whiter, then dissolved into whiteout. I remembered how vertigo felt when I had steered my airplane into fog or clouds.

The day, too, continuously lost more of its light. Snowflakes no longer hit the ground but raced horizontally against my windshield. Earlier I had installed chains. Fortunately, halfway up, I seemed to own the road. No other macho human had felt obliged to placate his stupidity.

I had a cell phone with me. If anything happened, I'd just call. On this mountain I learned firsthand how to spell the words *roaming* and *searching* and *no signal*.

The law forbids night driving with only the parking lights turned on. I did not care. Headlights were out of the question. With them in "on condition," I could not see ten yards in front of me, the car shifted automatically into the crawl gear.

Maybe I should have stayed home and watched the sliding panorama on television. The media sure had their ball. Not in a hundred years had the snow fallen this fast, this heavy. I read later in the paper the skiers at the slopes sixteen miles up the mountain had shushed down to the parking lot to snowed-in SUVs. Despite their all-powerful four-wheel-drives, they plugged the roads on their way home.

I finally reached the top at some 4,000 feet. The worst had passed. On the way down the snow fell in smaller flakes. The headlights reclaimed their job. I did not meet one oncoming car until I drove into Leavenworth shortly after 8 PM. After unwelding my hands from the steering wheel, I came to see how beautiful this little village had been dressed for the holidays.

Leavenworth around Christmas twinkles and glitters in a thousand lights of so many colors. German Christmas music, beer, sleigh rides, Sauerkraut and Knackwurst, wine, costumes, and Santa (more than one) ho-ho-hoing through the streets of this very busy place. People from all over come by train and bus, swarming this small Alpine town tucked between tall silent mountains.

*M*y cell phone woke up. I dialed my friends with whom I had planned to stay overnight in the larger metropolis of Wenatchee, some twenty miles down the flat but icy highway.

"Well, Claus, I'm glad to hear you begged off. The news just reported the pass closure. The DOT worried about possible avalanches—"

"Fred, hey, Fred, I am in Leavenworth. I—"

"You're where? No kidding! Crazy, that's what you are…"

His voice spoke of his fears.

"No message from you. We called you at home to let you know it's a no-good day to dare the pass."

"Forgive me, man. Piece of cake, that mountain. I think, though, I will stay at a hotel here. That way I do not tempt fate anymore today."

"Good idea. Eileen, at the moment, does not display her best social skill as a hostess. The dinner has shriveled. Looks like someone drove over the salad. You better send her some flowers, boy, if you ever want to visit her again.

What a guy, so stupid!" A small silence. "Yet…I would have been disappointed had you not tried, idiot!"

Next morning, I checked in at the KOHO station right on time. The interview went well. The host asked real questions to which I could respond intelligently. Several listeners called in with their own comments.

"…man, Claus, *Kreuznach*, how gruesome a vineyard…I been in the same camp. God, God…"

A woman later gave me this.

"Mr. Hackenberger, when you said forgiveness holds the key to a peaceful life, the basic ingredient of true love—well, you made me cry. Thank you."

Such a moment makes any day worthwhile, hands to me an exceptional reward, and so humbles me.

Along Highway 2, at the Books For All Seasons, I gave several short presentations followed by brisk sales. Pat, the store owner, ended the day with kind words.

"I have been watching you. You are a people magnet; they really like to listen to you. We will arrange for you to come back here soon. Yes?"

My modest take warmed my pocket on the way home. I knew getting an interview and a book signing, both in the same town, on the same day, and just before Christmas, had been a stroke of great good luck.

I had a short bite to eat at Krystal's. The place bulged with tourists. I ate in the bar standing, one foot up on the bottom railing. The bartender, Deedee, made time to chat.

"What brings you here? To do some shopping, watch the tree-lighting tonight?"

"I came here for a book signing across the street at Books For All Seasons"

"You wrote a book? Are you the fellow this morning on the radio? Oh yes, you sound like him. An author, oh my God, really! How much does a copy cost? I would like to buy one from you."

Such enthusiasm put a smile into my heart.

"Tell you what. I have one in my car. I'll sign it and let you have it for free."

Her eyes crinkled.

"Wow, nobody ever signed a book for me. You know, I'm quite the reader. Thank you, thank you, Claus."

I finished eating, retrieved a book from the trunk of the car, and wrote on the front page:

Deedee, have always peace in your heart.

She came around the bar, took the book, kissed the cover, and gave me a hug.

A whisper reached my ear.

"Could you stay for the night?"

For seconds did I look into her eyes and with my fingers did I touch her lips.

*D*ark.

I took my time to drive home.

Fairytale land! The once-again falling snow danced with my headlights. I stopped, turned off the engine, and cranked the window down. The parking lights came on and doused the crystal flakes in amber.

Cold air carried away my tiredness. Distanced from the tinsel, dressed-up trees and people, I let the silence calm.

I saw myself in another time, standing tall with orchestra and chorus, sending the Alleluia out into the majestic cathedral and the oncoming Holy Night.

My Christmas…truly joyful, truly filled with peace.

Search for Light

THIS TOP I MADE FOR YOU REMINDS ME OF LIFE. ONCE IN A WHILE WE HAVE TO GIVE IT A TWIRL.

Cheering up a friend whose wife underwent serious surgery.

Longing

The tall maple in front of my house is tired. So are the poplars along the River. Leaves, not quite golden yet, played with by the autumn wind, twirl to the ground.
It has been a hot and dry summer. Now, at the end of September, the River shows its sandy bed. Hardly any water trickles over its bottom. I cannot remember seeing such a scene the years before.
Uncertainty roams my heart. I feel change coming about, but not the inevitable turn of season that means the days soon grow shorter, the weather cooler, and the wind more ferocious.
No, a change my life will hand to me, put together with happiness and joy, or with unfortunate events. Fall allows those feelings of mine to sprout in the used soil the summer no longer cares for.
My emotions tick like a pendulum, side to side, to and fro. As I walked the River trail this morning, my partner, Littleman, stretched the long leash, craving rabbits and

squirrels. At times he froze and stared at a distant blackberry bush that had come alive caressed by the wind. He takes time to convince himself there are no mice or weasels ready to tease him. Sometimes he will come, when I remind him, but often I must drag him from his dream of creatures waiting to be chased. He catches up with me, running faster than a bullet whistling by. His short tail could be taken for a windshield wiper turned on high. He will stop in front of me, assuming a pose that catches me off guard again and again, melts my heart like chocolate in the sun.

He sits up, a soldier at attention, with his head tilted a little to his left. His black eyes ask—I can hear the silent query—*OK, man, what do we do next?*

Littleman, you are such a good dog. Yes, let's keep going.

With him, though, words are not enough. So, bending to him, I repeat my praise and scratch the behind of his ears. And the leash gets tight again.

But today, I am not quite with him. Thoughts of what the future might bring don't want to go away. The older I get the more weight do they seem to carry. I never have been afraid of change, of new things coming my way, but I do always worry. Why?

Whenever I had to open a new bag, I found not all tasted bitter. Sometimes I had to dig deep to find the candy, the sweet moments, even days bright and clear. To be true, I want to find love.

My life runs incredibly well, but I do not always fill my day. I am longing. I am very alone. Often I daydream walking along the River, holding her hand in mine, how would that feel? After an errand, being out among strangers, coming home to a warm hug, how would that be?

The ones who have been ordered to stack my bag always forget to pack this precious item—love.

Well, when I open this new bag just by chance I might find a hint, might go and look for a woman I could become friends with, could share time with.

I imagine this acquaintance not to be like times ago. Deeper, I am more aware that nothing belongs to me, on loan only, can be taken back at the blink of an eye. Deeper, I am less hard on yesterday and more aware of now. It would be good to know someone I could kiss.

For many years, biking used to be the time to recharge my senses. Early in the morning, rain or rising sun, I pedaled along the same trail nearly eight miles a day—9,485 miles altogether. The chain gears became as worn as an old man's teeth.

I often felt tempted to share my thoughts with this River. Sounds funny? Yes, in the beginning I thought of myself as being silly, maybe even deranged. But then I discovered this dialogue helped me process all kinds of questions.

The River listened, my most brutal critic. He gave me his opinion, balled me out, hissed out loud hearing my complaints. These waters never were good in praising me. "Atta boy!" did not come forth. As time went by, this River knew me well.

One day I had to leave in a hurry, had to go into surgery. My heart had given out and needed to be repaired. I did not have time to explain or even say goodbye to my River. I wrote a letter to him.

Foolish? Maybe. I did it any way.

> *River,*
> *far from you I walk across dry land*
> *had to leave*
> *no time to say farewell*
> *the road I am on feels dusty hot*
> *days and nights stretch, endless*
> *time does not want to rest*
> *River, I long for*
> *the trees on your banks*
> *to listen to your flowing to the sea*
> *your coves I miss*
> *the ducks and geese*
> *the rain*
> *the wooden bridge crossing you*

Two hard years kept me from my meandering friend. I so missed his tranquility, my drifting with him. Often, during my sad times, my mind followed his run down to the big lake. I imagined the fog floating close to the surface, remembered the early mornings before sunrise. I used to breathe the smell of wet grass, awaiting with him the birth of a new day.

I wanted to see him, to talk with him, to tell him I am still his friend. But I knew I had to wait.

Then, after some time, I felt change wanted to meet me.

I got better.

During the weeks I waited, I'd been thinking how to approach him. He might be angry I left him so suddenly, without a real goodbye. Maybe he needed a cheering, a wry story he could laugh at. I decided to tell him of a dream I'd had one night.

I went to touch the waters of my River.

"Hey, hey, River, not so fast, please! I must talk to you. I am restless. You are mad at me? So sorry. I have not been well for over two years. Jay, my friend, remember the good man who rode the bike with me all those years? I had asked him to let you know why I could not be here to see you.

"River, you and I talked a lot over the years. We helped one another and became soul friends. You listened to me, scolded me when I didn't want to drive all the way to the end of the trail. And on rainy days, when hardly anybody showed, I made you giggle with my jokes. I am thinking especially of your dry time, when you had hardly any water in your bed and you felt ashamed. I drove to keep you company.

"Sometimes, you saw me sit by the bridge, alone, crying. When this woman shredded my love – you remember – I asked you to take my tears to the ocean. Poseidon, you assured me then, would have his tall waves polish them and turn them into sparkling diamonds.

"Come, we are still friends, yes?"

His answer came loud and quick.

"Enough! Friends, of course, talk.

"Walk faster, though. See, how high my water flows along the dikes? Been that way for some time. Rain, rain, rain. The Lord must have scolded his Angels…"

"Yes, you are high all right, but what have angels to do with the rain?"

"Hey, Claus, you forgot? Raindrops fall when angels weep."

"My mother used to say—"

"Never mind your mama. Walk, man! This is my busy time. Tomorrow, the experts warn I might grow strong and wide, spill and march all over your town. Come on, run! Talk to me! I want to hear what new complaints you wear."

"Okay, I—"

"Faster, boy! Your heart, I know, it rebelled. You okay now?"

"Ya."

"So, what is going on in your life? The way you look, I wager you got hooked one more time by another beauty. No? Yes?"

"Well, 'hooked' sounds so streetish. I—"

"Man, you are eighty. Not that you look it, but see, your gait is that of a fellow who's been walking too far for too long. You shuffle like a penguin."

"Well, thank you. You still know how to hurt a fellow. River, hear me. I can hardly keep up. The way you speed around your bends. Jeez, it makes me dizzy. Whether I am old or not, I can still tell when a woman—"

"Hey, you funny fellow, you make me laugh. I happen to know you're not an expert when it comes to women. How old is she? Girl, woman, crone?"

"You'll find out a little later."

The River gurgled.

"Just as I thought…"

"Something new, not sure yet how it could be, welcomes me when I come home from errands at the grocer or the post office. As I walk into my living room I sense a good time might come my way. I am suspicious, Tinker Bell swirled through here. I found traces of sparkling dust all over the carpet."

"Hey, guy, you walk faster! I'm in a hurry. I have no time to wait to hear your story."

"Man, I'm almost running. Listen, for a few days now I feel lighter, whistle here and there. When I look into the mirror I see this joyful smile on my face, tinted deviously."

I had not expected such tender emotions to ever touch me again.

*I*t happened when I did not look. I had a book signing in Tukwila. She came by, wanted to know about my writing. That's how we met for the first time. One evening after work we had coffee together at one of those fancy places at Southcenter. She ordered a latte with some long name. I sipped steamed milk.

Sweet, soft, unpretentious, well-dressed, she looked at me with passionate eyes. Warm, natural, real. With both hands molded around her cup, she told me about herself and her job. Because the crowded coffee shop hummed like a beehive, I leaned over to hear her. I didn't say much about myself. She, by then, already had read both books and knew more about me than my mother ever did.

After a while I heard myself thinking: *I like you, Jessie.*

"We decided we would go for dinner one evening. I suggested the Icon Grille in Seattle, a fabulous place with food out of this world. Dale Chihuly, Seattle's world-famous glass artist, had decorated the restaurant with his enormous glass-blown arrangements."

"Oh boy, I hear it coming—deep love. I shiver."

"You what…?"

"I am kidding. Right, we rivers don't know of those things. But, hearing you talk, some old trees crack way down at the bottom of my bed."

"Crackling trees? That's nothing. Can't compare to what I felt."

"Oh…nothing, you say. I can tell they only fixed a small muscle in your chest. The inside of your heart, the doctors did not touch. Empathy still is not your strong side."

"My friend, go back to flowing, it's along the line of what you do best."

I am running by now, breathing harder. But I filled in the blank spots, told him I sent a bouquet of flowers to her office where she manages a small business.

She had whispered over the phone, "I like you too." Yes, I heard it that way.

"Sure you heard right?" The River asked.

And now I needed to let him know.

"River, River, my so cherished friend, I had only a dream, a wonderful dream I had to share with you."

Silence, the River did not answer. Only the whirlpools flushing his shoreline told me of his sadness.

New Ears

*I*n the lyrical words of Shania Twain:
"From this moment on..."
Whenever you send e-mail messages or letters, you no longer need to write so loud.

My first hearing aids are working in my ears. Computer-controlled—adjustable, digital, and completely wireless—they actually talk to each other.

"The installer," Greg, a kind and knowledgeable young man, fit them into my ears. Strange, foreign, uncomfortable!

"Say something," he suggested.

"Well, let's see..." I know, a funny expression under the circumstances.

I turned around to find the person who just had spoken these three silly words. I found nobody else in the room. I thought, "That couldn't have been my voice!" But, wooee! Claus had just spoken with his new hearing "things" in place. I could not recall ever talking so loudly, being so articulate!

Leaving the establishment, I followed a fellow whose shoes hit the tile floor so hard, so noisily, it half scared me to keep walking behind him. I halted, let him make space between us. On the way down the elevator stairs I heard the whole mechanism gasping for lubrication. I won't mention what I felt walking through those tall glass doors on the way out. I looked back, hoping the big bang had not broken them.

Crossing the lane to get to where my car waited for me, a Lexus honked at me. I jumped.

Back in my car, Littleman, my sweet dog right away discovered something smelled new and different. But he did not seem to mind my loud-speaker greetings.

Honestly, I had forgotten turn-signal blinkers shout, "Tick! Tick! Tick!" as they support the flashing green arrow head. I turned the radio on to listen to the news. The volume, sitting at where I had it for years, almost made me drive off the road.

Woooeee!!!

Why did I wait so long?

To celebrate, Doggie and I went to the beach. On the way I bought a pretzel for lunch and a chunk of sausage we both like.

Low tide, yet I could hear the lapping the small waves whispered visiting the shore. We ate, were happy. The brown paper bag exploded into my ear when I crunched it into a ball. A crowing crow buzzed us. It could have been an F14, sure sounded like one.

OK, the TV and my radio/CD volumes at my home have been adjusted. But the noises outside and in my house challenged my security.

For quite some time had I not heard all these tiny winky-dinky knocks and rumbles. Closing the bathroom door seemed to shatter the whole establishment, scared me some at first. Well, yes, everything blasted refreshed amplitudes through my brain. When I closed the lid of the toilet, I thought I had busted the whole fixture. I also discovered all hinges allowing my doors in the house to swing needed oil in a very bad way.

Why, by George, did I feel insecure?

Let me drag in a parallel experience I had when the coal mine's elevator dropped me off at nine thousand feet down the shaft. Noise I did not know existed hit me from all angles, the swishing of the high-speed coal belts, the clatter the electric carts made, the hissing manmade wind, the chilling squeals in the wooden shoring...

At least now I had daylight in my house so I could see these ghosts or monsters breathing hard in my quarters. My bedroom window stays open overnight. Yes, I can hear now the rain drumming on my roof.

*I*t took a while to get used to those elevated frequencies, yet I felt like I walked around in a new world.

I skipped dinner that evening. My stomach shook ever so slightly. The day had been very fascinating, all in all an overwhelming experience!

*T*he next day I filed the invoice for these remarkable apparati. I retrembled. I could have bought half of a new car with that money! But, what a way to hear! And I must add I now feel safer. And, please, tell your keyboard to keep from clicking that loudly.

Driftwood

This morning's storm passed, took its bulging clouds east to the mountains. The ebb tide drew the breakers back into the ocean. Bouncing driftwood, not quite finding the right spot to run aground, battered the shore. The far horizon promised calmer weather, a good time for me to walk the beach.

I saw a giant bird that escaped the sea millions of years ago, leaving behind whale and shark and ray. His wings, not feathered, but of twisted roots bleached by sun and salt, still want to soar. His ferocious beak, the gruesome face, the curved body, taller than I, must have scared the dinosaurs.

I went to touch this wet body. Though he did not move, I felt him shiver.

Can you tell me how those drifted trees die into living shapes?

Search for Light

Claus Hackenberger

GOD, ONE WAY OR ANOTHER, IS ALWAYS AROUND. TO ME, THOUGH, SOMETIMES I PLAY HIDE AND SEEK WITH HIM.

Answering a question during a speech at Seattle University

At the Mall

Saturday afternoon, under a gray sky, I drove across town to buy bread and sausage at my favored delicatessen in Burien. As I traveled back on I-5, the highway afforded an astounding peripheral view of the massive layout Southcenter Shopping City occupies. Thousands of acres are loaded with blots of merchant buildings separated by open space parking lots, streets, and multi-floor garages.

A sea of cars, red roofs on wheels—yellow, blue, some black, some white too, covered every conceivable square foot of free space. Relentless rains had washed the colored mosaic to a shine, making the cars look like they just had arrived from Detroit.

In between the vehicles people floated back and forth. The parking lot feeders crawled with incoming and outgoing shoppers. A fascinating, living picture, changing moment by the moment in silent slow motion, ebbing and flowing through the tiny spaces between the multi-colored rectangles.

While I kept gazing, the exit to Renton buzzed by, and the traffic sucked me right into this swarm of park-less automobiles.

I let fate talk me into visiting this city of commerce.

Like a dog circling the spot where he will nap, I drove in circles until I finally found a space I decided I could squeeze into. I kissed Littleman, my doggy, closed the door, and pushed the lock-button on my key. The car beeped its confirmation. But, as always, I worried whether the door locks were clever enough to deter dog thieves—unthinkable.

Far away, the JC Penney's building hovered, seemingly touching the horizon.

Westfield's food court crawled with old and young. No vacancy. Moving with and against the crowd, I elbowed with young, pierced generations—some whose ears dangled dancing earrings, others whose lobes stretched with penny-size silver washers. Smoky green-grass odor escaped from under some windbreakers. Pants hung low on hips let me see blue-green alligator tattoos peaking over the belt line.

A haircut here and there could have improved the appearance of security guards helplessly embedded in this stagnant mass.

From India and Africa, the Far East, women dressed in beautiful, brightly colored gowns pushed strollers through the dragging mingle. Men wearing turbans and long beards loudly chatted away in their undecipherable dialects. Wherever I looked people chewed pizza.

I entered the video store and bought *Lord of the Dance*. The young lady validating my credit card wore a sparkling diamond at the tip of her tongue.

I noticed two young soldiers in fatigues standing in line for a taco and a coke. Out of nowhere my memory flashed across my inner screen. Though I did not hurt, I remembered the pain.

What had me want to mill with the crowd? A need to be "with." I felt lost that day, lonely, out of the loop, feeling my chipped tooth in the gears of changing times.

In the past, whenever Renton Town came too close to me, I took my motorcycle to the road. I went visiting friends in southern Oregon, tooling along the coast of the Pacific Ocean, or climbing far and high up in Washington's mountains. Always the consistent beauty of nature assured my trust in the future and strengthened my self-confidence. Coming home from those trips, I brought back with me a refreshed perspective allowing me to reassess the values I judged life by. And some times during my journeys I even found a new piece to fit my puzzle I kept working on. Pure sunsets, cool moon-lit nights, still silence, starred heavens all offered peace in abundance.

Older now by years I often think of those golden moments and try to feel the tranquility those hours once let me touch.

Hey, you! Claus, hello! Man, you have to go home.
I should not leave Littleman alone in the car. Someday, someone might like his looks, perhaps break the window and steal him. Although that tiny fear lived always in the back of my mind, this day it knocked on

my chest. There still lives in me residual violence. I knew what I would be capable of if anyone would harm my Littleman.

Hurrying through rain and blasting wind I searched to find my car. I remembered only that I had parked near the river, quite far away from the shopping hive. Fortunately the new bed sheets I had bought at JC Penney wore a plastic bag that kept them from getting wet. I was not as well dressed. My parka did not fancy a hood, and rain rinsed down my back. My eyeglasses needed wipers. Rivulets of rainwater blurred my vision. I pushed the search button on the key but heard no answer from my car.

Somebody stole the Malibu?

My iced, bare hands turned numb. The jeans clung to my thighs.

Not yet panic, but frantic, yes! Littleman, oh God, my Littleman! What am I to do? I have no Plan B. My eyes darted about helplessly. No, not the car over there, I walked by already twice. Not mine. The wind had me shiver. I leaned over the trunk of the car next to me, deposited the Penney sheets on its lid, and closed my eyes.

Think!

Wow, did I leave through the same door I had come in? When I opened my eyes I saw J C's building at a different quarter of a turn angle than I remembered when I had arrived. Shit! What could have me so very screwed up?

I grabbed the plastic bag and ran, never mind the puddles. Breathing hard I pulled open the door to Penney's. Shedding water all over I hurried by surprised customers in search of the "ninety degree" exit to my right. Feeling spatially disorientated I dragged the sheet bag over the carpeted floor. Frightened bystanders were convinced they watched a fleeing shoplifter. They called home; the evening news would show clips taken by the security cameras, But the corpulent security force did not get a hold of me.

The day had given way to a bleary evening, though I did make out the river in the distance. Racing closer I again hit that sonar button on the key. The Malibu answered. I put the bed sheets on top of the car and with fumbling fingers open the door.

Halleluiah!

Littleman squealed and licked my face ferociously. Everything inside the car went wet. I climbed in quickly and slammed the door shut. The windows had been blinded by his happy, hurried doggy breaths.

I hugged that black ball. How I did hug him.

A short drive and we were home. He rushed for the water bowl while I changed into dry wear. Both of us ate dinner and went to watch TV.

I could not quite concentrate. Something appeared to be amiss. Before I went to bed I thought of unfolding J C's sheets just to feel that 450 thread count.

They weren't in the car. I checked the trunk twice. They weren't in the ante room, in my workshop, in my house.

No more Saturdays at the mall, I promised Littleman.

Love

evening
street lights teased
the stars to wake
you stayed
shared your night

The summer seems to have run out of all the warm weather it had in store for the year. Mornings are cooler now. Often gray fog lingers through the early hours of the day.

Yet this evening pleasantly settles over these pastures the river nourishes. I stride atop its bank in thoughts of our discussion last night.

Roxann hesitated. Love...she wonders if she really knows this deep inside, warm feeling. She asked how this emotion could embrace people.

I promised I would think about an explanation, maybe even come up with an answer. The harder I tried, the more I discovered I might not be able to rest her uncertainty.

I love you.

These three words vibrate, spoken in innumerable languages, dressed in myriad expressions, weave the fabric of Life. Love, I believe, empowers my life, keeps me fulfilled, allows me to give and share from the innermost hiding places in my soul.

I love you.

Love might flicker like a match struck to flame in the dark. Love might explode with deafening thunder and hit with the crackle of lightning. Timidly, Love can set a night aglow, barely kindling a very new day only to strike quicker than a cobra, leaving its burning, yet so sweet poison, in our hearts.

I love you.

Intimate whispers offer all and more, erupting from deepest feelings. Love gives, yet wants to be caressed. Love needs response, must be given permission to touch.
Falling in Love, there is no day like any other, but I cannot explain why or how this falling happens.

I love you.

How many times in my life did I say…
I did not know your name, never had I seen you before, yet I heard your voice, found your eyes asking me to halt.
And how many times did I fall in Love, jump off safe ground with the bungee cord unfastened from my harness, hoping the woman would hold me? Over time I learned these three words might not always be written in

permanent ink, but could fade into dark emptiness without notice.

I love you.

Those three words also may wear ragged gowns, tailored by man, held together with ropes braided in greed and ill will. Man kills in the name of Love.

I love you.

Roxann, I cannot even come close and see the center of this beautiful, phenomenal soul moment when two people fall in Love. Only might I say to love means to dare Life, to embrace Life with every moment time shares with us.

Without Love, I believe we could not walk this earth.

Just Moments

…so very long ago…

A full moon glazed the Columbia River with liquid silver. Only ripples shivering its surface told the mighty stream did live. I halted, got out of my car, and stepped into the bleached twilight.

Across the road, I halfway stumbled at the guardrail as I scurried down to the edge of the river. Like magic, the silver surface changed into millions of glittering crystals.

Cars raced by above. The high bank muffled their hurry. Silence, only the waters talked. My watch showed no time. The moon had slowed its orbit. Nothing moved but the river.

*M*y day had been long, wonderful at that, rewarding and fulfilling. The dewed grass felt soothing. I leaned back and an endless sky above took my wish. With my eyes closed, I let go.

Yet time woke too soon. To soon the moon took up its journey. Too soon the silver and crystals faded into the night.

And so the river had gone to rest.

*D*riving home over the pass, I thought of what we had shared only a few hours before. I did miss being near you.

After my radio interview in Chelan, we met for dinner. I listened. Not all your life had been woven on Sundays.

*W*e walked arm in arm across the parking lot to our cars. You looked at me. When you kissed me I felt your tears. But you turned into the night. I knew you had left forever.

Know, please know, those precious moments did not leave. They kept living with me through the many years. I still at times touch you in my dreams.

Where, Megan, where are you?

now

my sun
the ocean
my wind
the clouds
my life
and the
rivers whisper

be and be and be
now
and love

Fall

A gray sky, uncertain of the rising sun, hovers over the streets of my town. This morning differs from the many mornings I have awakened to in recent days.

M aple trees along the river, which only yesterday seemed so lush and leafy green, have turned a golden hue Midas himself would covet. Some leaves show off splashes of ruby-red the dew has polished to a lustrous gleam. Cold and damp, the breeze continually shifts the shape of the bushes near the water. Wild geese drag frightening cries low over harvested land. Clouds hasten the heavens hanging full with rain. I button the collar of my coat and push my chilled hands deep into the warm pockets of my trousers.

*C*areless and lazy the river drifts from bend to bend, slow, a tired snake of brown silt. Low water gives daylight to rotting tree trunks sucked into the dark bottom. Contorted branches, black and bare, beg for the leaves the wind has taken from them. Despite the cold and rushing clouds, I find a comforting place to sit halfway up the river's bank. I hold onto my knees with both of my arms and look at a once regal tree, now a rotten trunk cemented in mud.

*T*his giant has witnessed better times up in the mountains reaching for the sky, carrying life through winters and blazing summers, daring dangerous thunderstorms, raging fires, blanketing snow. Perhaps shifting earth tumbled it into the water to a death by drowning. The old tree, embedded for all time to come, reminds me of monstrous lizards crawling through the same mud before the ice put them to sleep.

*D*rifting grass and tangled twigs have formed tiny islands towering midstream. A blue heron stands on one, still, cast in this motionless moment of a frigid day. A gull floats by trailing three freshly born ducklings. I chuckle.

*V*ery near, ahead, a bank of fog wallows towards me, unexpected. I think to turn back, too late. It engulfs me. I breathe the pale air. Sheer veils ghost by. The mist parts to let me through, then swirls together again behind my back. Poplars nearby, bleached, blur into tall gothic shadows. No longer can I see the river.

*S*ilence.

*T*ime stills, and I give in.

Search for Light

Lost You

glittering quartz, life, ran through our hands
day and night we searched for answers
from heaven, from friends

love   share
they told us
we did

but you could not stay

leaving in your wake…

tears
where laughter once lived

pain
where care once healed

darkness
where light once reigned

emptiness
where love once filled our days

Birthday Wishes

for your birthday
I wish I could bring precious gifts
find tall words
give sunny skies
and joy and happiness
to you

I wish I could take you to gardens
where flowers blossom the year around

I wish we could sail to distant islands
dive for pearls
play with dolphins in the surf

I bring my love
garnished with the star
I picked last night from heaven

Empty

Days woke damp and cold.
The sun would rise, shine its warmth on me.
But I could not see, did not feel it.

Days woke in pain, in despair.
I remembered life had a reason for me to be
But I did not believe anymore.

Days woke with hollowed emptiness.
Days woke without hope.
Days woke without light.
Days woke without God.

One night with my eyes shut,
I reached for my gun.
I felt it heavy and cold as ice.
I never had been that close.
I kissed my little dog and hugged him.
I hugged him. I hugged him.

Medicine did not help.
I could not make it work.
The tall mirror in my bedroom scared me.
I took it down.
I reeked of fear, desolation, uncertainty
No soap and water could wash away.

There were other days
Somewhat lighter, yet beyond my control.
More than two years needed to pass
Until I found myself.

One morning, the day woke and
Set me free,
Handed back to me my laughter,
My joy, my confidence.
My life and I were one again.

But I did not know whether the hour would last...

Littleman, my black toy poodle, sat in my lap as I drove south on Highway 167. Dr. G. had requested my presence for a checkup of my heart he had repaired two years back.

I parked the car on Level B in the Health Center's garage and tried to calm my shivering dog. His eyes begged me not to leave him alone. He yelped as I walked from the car. I believe without this loving animal I would not have made it.

The kind doctor, stethoscope hanging pendulously from his neck, radiated quiet strength. His so gentle eyes rested on mine. He took my fear. I felt the warmth in his words when he asked me to let go.

Think of the bright colors you sculpt your work with, Claus. Live your art. Keep writing. You're not there yet. You still have a long road ahead of you.

His hug at the end of our meeting I took with me as his assurance this life still needs me.

I am using our hug as the center stone of the new arch I am building, stone by stone.

p.s. Dr. G., I wrote these pages for you, especially for you. I see no better way to thank you for saving my life. These lines allow me to share with many, young and old, my humble gratitude. Thank you!

Search for Light

Claus Hackenberger

Graves will never go away. That pain is in our hearts to stay.

Going on is what I take with me from those wet lawns. Going on is what I am trying to do, sharing love they no longer can give.

In a conversation with a friend in pain after visiting her daughter's grave.

Search for Light

friend

today
sunshine
wraps my greeting
the blue ribbon
I borrowed from the sky
let me share
this beautiful morning
bearing our tomorrow
let me share with you
a moment in peace and in love

Night

Night needs the day to fade
To come alive

Night needs no door
To enter my house

Night need not ask
To settle in my room

Night needs silence
To usher in peace

Night I need
To rest
To dream
To be whole again

goodbye

have forgotten your name
will think of you no more
no pain darkens my day

for years I carried water for you
at times the crock got chipped
today it broke, fell back into the well

stood there stunned
cried
in time I will heal
never will I be hurt again

Without You

Lord,

your help I need

    to face this moment

    to let him go

    to say farewell

    to touch his stone

    to dare tomorrow

Lord

your help I need

    to walk alone

May 18, 1992
Our son Tommy
left us.

Last Time

last time I looked, evening settled in
last time I listened, rain rolled off my roof
water fled down the gutter

last time I thought of you, I felt pain
last time I stood still, the ocean's breakers
hurled drifted trunks onto the beach

last time I stared into the mirror, I saw tired eyes
last time I picked blossoms for you, they wilted
could not find water for them to drink

last time I loved you, I felt betrayed
I wakened through nights, missing you
waited to hear the knock on my door

last time I wrote a letter to you, the envelope came back
you no longer lived there, the notice said
dawn after dawn birthed endless days, all of hurt

last time I looked, the sky broke into blue
a sun warm and gentle touched me
kissed the flowers near my house

no longer do I need to look into yesterday

Search for Light

Claus Hackenberger

I FIRMLY BELIEVE FORGIVENESS IS THE KEY TO A NEW TOMORROW.

In an interview at KOMO 4 TV in Seattle

at the cemetery

silent snowflakes drift
cling to tall trees in my yard
dress bushes with glitter
white and soft

tossed by gusts
the snow weaves a blanket
covers graves and stones
blots dates and names

flakes thaw in my tears
drip into my praying hands

silent snowflakes drift
fill prints my shoes have made
as I went to leave the hill

Take my hand.

A silver moon glazes the flowers sleeping, dreaming in their beds around my house. The river curls its way down to the lake. Frogs and fish have gone to rest. The evening waking, urges the day to leave. Peace settles with the dark.

but then
morning brings unbearable pain
man again has destroyed life

gutters turn red

three hundred people are dead
half of them children

tears so many tears

take my hand   I ask you   take my hand
I am afraid

death is catching life

take my hand   take my hand
help me not to remember
I am afraid

gruesome   chilling
life is leaving

take my hand   I beg you   take my hand
I am afraid
help me pray

Tommy

*N*ovember 2002

My books, A LONG WALK and *the river*, had been on the shelves at various book stores for a just little over a year when I received the invitation. Would I come to Chelan to give an interview? Dennis Rahm at radio station KOZI wanted to talk to me up close and personal.

Green author that I was, I embraced this opportunity to share my thoughts with so many people. Nervous, yes! But invaluable to me, and I hope enlightening to others.

Later at the River Walk Bookstore, I signed copies and received an audience wanting to know how I survived Hitler and his war. Libby, the owner, made me feel like an *NY Times* best seller. A gift—to exchange conversation and philosophies with such open, interesting patrons.

As evening approached, the crowd dwindled, so that when a woman came in, I noticed her immediately.

Friendly, attractive, warm, she appeared to be in her late forties. Libby knew her and introduced me. Maria.

"Hackenberger?" she said as she took my hand. "I went to school with a Hackenberger. Oh, my God, don't tell me! You are related to that good-looking Tom from Edmonds High?"

"Tom, yes, Tom, my second son."

"Oh my God! You are Claus. Of course, I know you too! Tom's father here in Chelan? Gracious God!"

Time switched to rewind. In seconds I relived those years. I bet Tommy stood right there next to me. Yes, I know he did.

"We all loved him. What a guy to be with! Our best quarterback. His music on the piano always took me away, so beautiful. So cute, so soft, and yet so strong—he could reach anything he wanted, our Tom, our hero."

And then the inevitable question that can never be answered.

"Why? Why did he have to leave so early in his life?"

We reminisced old times and new. Maria told me of friends who had moved forward in life, who had married, were raising families, had found their way.

The lake reflected the oncoming night. I did not use the shortcut but the long route to my home. Time still hesitated to move the hands on my watch.

Halfway through the treacherous Blewett Pass, I halted at the side of the road. Rain hammered my windshield. Gusts pushed against my car.

"Lord, why do you do this to me?" I screamed from the top of my lungs.

That phone call had reached me at work.
Our Tommy died this morning...
Once again, it busted into the open. Yesterday raced to be now, yesterday with all its dark might, its pain, its forever torture.
Why?

Missing him knows no time.

I miss you

   wednesday evening

     behind snow-covered mountains a tired sun sinks
      into the sea

      my windows are wide open

       sweet scent from my neighbor's lilac

        lives with me in my house

        soon dusk will lure the night to wake

         for us to rest and dream
         of yester time
         of tomorrow
         of life and of love

Amber,

I just heard. I am most happy for you!

How do I tell what I mean to say?
My sentences, what do I fill them with?
Where do I find the words so all my greetings,
all my wishes bring sunshine, peace, and love into your new life?
Saying yes to one another,
I want you, I am yours,
makes the hour ring with love.

A little older now, we know those simple words
carry meanings
far deeper than we understood in our younger years.
They summon a new life, filled with expectations,
with sharing the future together.

I trust you and you can trust me –

where else does this still exist but in the promise two
people give each other?

I wish your new bond makes you whole, nourishes
your dreams...
And that peace always lives in your hearts.

my friends

time moves on
a new year
2008

I hope each of us will accept every day as a gift
I wish you and I will keep believing in tomorrow
but know we live now   need to forgive yesterday

I hope we will own every moment we create
I wish us to think of those without means
and give to them to lessen their pain

I hope we will embrace both blue sky and dark clouds
I wish we will stay healthy   reach our goals
keep peace and love growing in our hearts
greetings

Search for Light

Winning comes in small packages wrapped in heavy paper.
Chatting with someone who did not want to understand winning is hard to accomplish

Willows Weeping

Whip-like branches hang straight down from hidden boughs above. An early spring dressed these wooden threads in coats sewn with tiny oval leaves – a green curtain the low afternoon sun sets aglow. These willows wear skirts made of long grass swaying in the gentle drift of air.

Standing close at the river's edge, I feel the breeze softly wrinkling its face. The word *creek* better describes this narrow stream, for it cannot be wider than fifty feet. The large lake that awaits its arrival swallows it whole.

Across, amidst fresh-green undergrowth, a pair of geese hides heads under their wings. Black helldivers leave intersecting wavelets as they dive into the murky waters. Once in a while small fish jump, wiggle, fall back. I see the splash they make, but no longer can I hear the swish when they disappear.

Tiny birds pick tiny bugs from the soil. Gulls and swallows zoom from highs down to barely inches above the water. Big black crows scream at each other from the bare branches of still budding trees.

I remember the sounds, the cooing, the twitter and tweet, the chirp these birdies fill the air with. When I hold my ears forward with both of my hands I can still get this jitter, but otherwise only the wind caught under my hood, makes the sound for this moment.

I find a bench facing the water, near the willows. The breeze, a little stronger now, teases the green skirts. Kauai comes to mind, the Polynesian hula, yes, this here swaying back and forth…

So good, I still can reach the days long since gone, can remember the island's evening suns pouring fires onto the horizons of endless oceans, white breakers foaming with gold. Yes, and in my mind I still can touch the distant stars and catch myself thinking about the universe.

And nowadays, walking with my dog I take time to look at what other surprises spring may have dreamed up overnight. I pluck white blossoms from the cherry trees in the park like I own them.

Strange, I feel time passes faster now, though some good moments seem to stretch, hang around longer than they used to. Not in school did they tell me, nor did life itself ever let on how long I must walk to find the light, how far before my way will crumble.

See, these willows made me wander off to places I had not intended to visit today. I rather meant to share a story my mother told when I still could hold up one hand to confirm I am five as we walked along another river growing its own willows. What she said stayed with me all those years. Why, I have asked myself, why can I never forget this story?

A toddler once played in the sand near a creek. Two ducks squabbled downstream, not far away. The little boy thought they were fighting and perhaps wanted to calm them. He waded into the stream. His mother saw him slip and go under.

Further down the creek the willow trees heard the mother's begging cries. They hurriedly knotted their branches, made a net, and dipped it into the rushing waters trying to fetch the boy. But the current had taken the child to the deep.

My mother answered before I could ask.

Yes, that's why these willows along rivers still have their branches touch the water. They keep mourning, weeping because they did not save the little boy. Don't you get too close to the river...

*W*henever I see willows weeping, whether near to me along my path or in a distant landscape I cannot help but watch my mind's rerun of that story.

Why?

I am not willing to keep on mourning for what I lost—family, friends, myself at times. Nothing can I change. Nothing can I bring back no matter how much I miss, regret, wish, pray. I believe mourning does not heal but hinders the message the past wants to be heard.

Sure, sometimes I still cry when I think of my son, Thomas – though not in the context of then but of now, without pain but my accepting the brutality of life.

Willows weeping – their tears stayed with me ever since my mother had told the story.

When an ugly war blasted those graceful trees into splinters, they no longer could reach for the bodies floating by in rivers death had tinted dark red.

Could I find another reason, not so sad, why willow limbs reach to touch the river?

Perhaps some time, long ago, the earth shifted a little and the river's flow diminished to a trickle. To quench their thirst, the trees let down their branches to drink from that slender thread of life. Even though the river once again filled its banks, the willows left their limbs hanging long forever after – just in case.

And so they have remained – strong and supple and enduring. As I watch, I think they do not only weep but also relish their hypnotic dance with the wind,

> *Cedars, firs, my trees are tall, arch into the sky*
> *like the priest's arms blessing the crowds*
> *when he says*
> *ite missa est*
>
> *though*
> *nothing ended   nothing waned*
>
> *endless time births life   endless love crafts peace*
> *man keeps searching for light*

... last page

The old man pulls the curtain aside and looks at the gray, rainy day the weatherman on Channel 7 had predicted the night before. Not certain of what he sees he moves his eyes closer to the pane searching right and left, hoping he would see the sun through the wet branches, motionless, sagging from the tall fir in his yard.

A harsh blast of wind drums heavy rain against the window. Startled, he lets go of the printed cotton and sits back on the bed. His left hand rubs his chin and makes him feel his stubbly cheeks. He no longer shaves as often as he did when he still worked.

Haphazardly he fluffs the two pillows at the head of the bed. He tries to read the green numbers on the Timex travel clock. He fumbles for his glasses—only 7:45. It will be a long day.

He used to be the man who most often ran around holding two candles, both lit at either end. Those whom he worked with remember him as an honest, fair companion, compassionate. After so many years have gone by, they still tell me he cared about people, their problems and happiness. The extra mile he ran had always been longer than the one of others. He did well at the job. They called him "C-H"—those simple letters of the alphabet. His real name is Claus, Claus Hackenberger, the engineer.

He retired after he hit sixty-seven. Cancer owned him for a while and in 2004, surgeons installed a new valve in his heart.

For a long time, then, he did not move the curtain at all to check what the day would be like. He knew—knew it would stay dark. Depression had taken over his daily routines, had made him be very unlike his customary self.

Despite suicidal ideations he kept on wanting to live, to heal. And today, he feels as good as he possibly could have expected. The hard times, though, did not give back all of his "C-Hness." Those up and down months changed his response to life.

Claus had asked me to come by the next time I surfaced in Seattle. He did not say why.

I had flown in late and overnighted close to where he lives. I called him and offered to buy lunch, but he didn't seem to be in the mood. He would have to take a nap before our meet at his house in the afternoon.

I should introduce myself and say where I met Claus for the first time. We both then were very young and entrenched in the apocalyptic killing spree in which Hitler had forced our guilty participation.

I am Paul Berck—same age, same height, same philosophy on life. Perhaps you have heard the name before.

Claus looks good sitting there in his leather chair, leaning back, a beige blanket wrapped around his legs. Littleman, the black poodle, lazily stretches on his lap. The small, carpeted living room fashions soft-light painted walls. Three large floor-to-ceiling windows invite lawn and flowerbeds inside. His daughter, Christine, he tells me, decorated his home with various pieces of his art.

I feel warm and very comfortable, cozy, on his loveseat couch, sipping "bubble-water"—club soda, that is—from a coffee mug.

*H*e stares at my shoeless feet.
"You remember, Paul, in that camp, when we took our boots off? We had worn them continuously for all of April. It wasn't until the end of May when we finally emancipated our feet..."

Freezing nights had puffed up our toes in dark blue.

*T*he old man does most of the talking. His mentioning the boots at first worries me. Would we rehash the past he so often had explained to me vanished many years ago?

...I am over it, no more pain. I have forgiven myself, time, and all who hurt us...

He wrote this sentence over and over. He spoke such words in interviews on radio and television. Their meaning he engraved in his writings, printed in his books he had published in recent years.

But no, I should have known, should not have worried.

We took on the moment, the present hour, what it might have in store for tomorrow. Still, I could hear in between the lines an uncertainty about this tomorrow. How much longer will he be able to push aside the curtain at daybreak? Can he finish forging what he has started to form? Love, Peace?

And of course, the universe comes up and his dire effort to comprehend its birth. He realizes he can not embrace even a small part of this larger-than-infinite All. He marvels at this timeless expanse and talks of buckyballs and nanotubes.

The afternoon has gone, though he does not need light to keep on sharing. No clock could ever tell how far the night has progressed. He sounds tired, slowing our discussion. Silence interrupts his voice. Silence stays with us.

The soft glimmer of the sodium streetlight near his house allows me to see he has fallen asleep. Our talk has ended. I feel his peace reaching for me.

When I get up the dog in his lap but stirs. I step outside. On the way to my car I press my shoes into my chest. Still raining, windy…

Tomorrow?

Last page?

I don't think so.

Index

... last page 145
A Few Days Before Christmas 15
Amber, 136
At Safeway's 26
At the Beach 73
at the cemetery 130
At the Mall 100
Birthday Wishes 117
Christmas 23
Code 4 50
Darkness 76
Driftwood 97
Empty 118
Fall 111

Search for Light

Forgive Me 43

friend 123

goodbye 125

If I Could Write 11

Just Moments 108

Last Time 127

Leavenworth 77

Life 40

Littleman 7

Longing 85

Lost You 115

Love 105

my friends 137

New Ears 93

Night 124

Peace 25

people people people 39

Prologue Changing Tides 1

Sometimes at Night 66

Take my hand. 131

Time 48

Tommy 132

Willows Weeping 141

Without You 126

I miss you 135